ANZIO

GREAT BATTLES OF
HISTORY

HANSON W. BALDWIN

General Editor

Also by Martin Blumenson

BREAKOUT AND PURSUIT
THE DUEL FOR FRANCE, 1944

ANZIO: THE GAMBLE THAT FAILED

MARTIN BLUMENSON

J. B. LIPPINCOTT COMPANY
PHILADELPHIA & NEW YORK

TO

MY MOTHER

AND FATHER

CONTENTS

MAPS

drawn by B. C. Mossman

A gamble that succeeds
is a bold stroke of genius.
A gamble that fails
is a foolhardy venture.

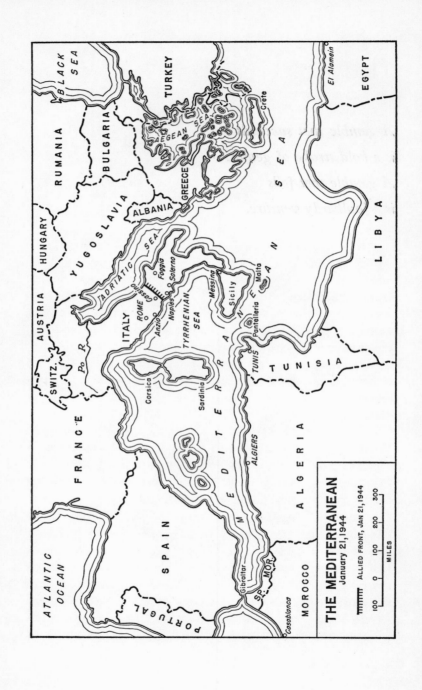

THE MEDITERRANEAN
January 21,1944

ⅢⅢⅢⅢ ALLIED FRONT, JAN 21,1944

100   0   100   200   300
MILES

THE ADVERSARIES

1 Anzio is a small town beside the sea, an hour's drive from Rome. It is a pleasant place. There are no monuments to visit, no tombs or relics to revere, no grand views, not even a restaurant of note. Only the beaches for sunbathing and digging in the sand, the cool blue water for swimming.

A prosperous seaport twenty-five hundred years ago, a fashionable summer resort two thousand years ago, entirely deserted a millennium ago, Anzio was the arena for a great clash of arms in 1944.

During four long months of that year the combatants of World War II were locked at Anzio in a deadly embrace.

The Allies threw down the challenge when American and British troops came ashore at Anzio in search of Rome. Picking up the challenge, the Germans reacted violently.

In the ensuing battle, the antagonists fought over a piece of ground. But more was at stake than the ground or Rome. The danger to each adversary was of such magnitude that the outcome of the war itself seemed to hang in that moment on the courage, skill, and stamina of those who struggled near the water's edge. This was the reason for the agony at Anzio.

In some respects the Anzio invasion was perhaps inevitable, destined for execution almost from the beginning of the combat in Italy. From the moment the Germans decided to contest the Allied advance from Naples to Rome, the Allied decision was as good as made. In a country where the fighting front could be no longer than the 80-mile width of the Italian peninsula, in a region where rugged mountains inhibited maneuver and favored the defense, in a campaign where the resources were sharply restricted—the Allies could look forward to no quick progress. To battle up the Italian mainland meant high losses and troop exhaustion with no clear prospect of success.

In this situation there was only one feasible way to get to Rome—go around the opposition by water. If, of course, the means for doing so were at hand—and adequate. If enough troops, enough boats, enough supplies could be spared from the main battle and moved quickly in an amphibious envelopment deep into the enemy rear.

Though probably inevitable, Anzio was a gamble. And in that sense, the Anzio operation was an aberration. The decision was reached in a curious manner, with impatience the basic motive and haste the characteristic quality of the conception.

For Anzio was the result, in large measure, of resentment and conflict between allies. The seed of Anzio was a difference of opinion, and the seed was nourished on long-term argument.

The United States and Great Britain had long been friends. The friendship between these governments deepened in the 1930s as the internal tyranny and external aggressions of the Fascist and Nazi dictatorships in Italy and Germany and the brutal military incursions of Japan into China revolted the American and British people.

The crushing victories of Germany during the early part of World War II drew the United States ever closer to Britain. The German invasion of Poland to start the war in 1939, the division of Poland between Germany and Russia, the German conquest of Norway and Denmark in 1940, the overrunning of the Netherlands, Belgium, and Luxembourg and the climactic German triumph over France in the same year, the entry of Italy into the war on the German side when French defeat was certain—these events left Britain standing alone but undaunted to defy the power of Germany. At that time British and Americans formed an unofficial alliance. Military leaders of both nations visited each other's capitals, exchanged information, and learned to work together.

In 1941, when Germany, instead of invading the British Isles, turned eastward and attacked the U.S.S.R., the British and Russians found themselves facing a common foe. In December of that year, when the Japanese bombed Pearl Harbor and after Germany and Italy declared war on the United States, the opponents of World War II stood arrayed. Despite earlier Anglo-American resentment against the Russians for their war with Finland, the Americans, British, and Russians formed a loose coalition.

Within that coalition, the Anglo-American alliance quickly crystallized into a close partnership. Bound together by mutual interests, a common language, like traditions, and the same enemies, the United States and Great Britain formed a partnership as close as any coalition in the history of warfare and politics.

Yet it was the divergent strategic interests of Britain and the United States and their continuing low-key disagreement on a fundamental question of how to conduct the war in Europe that prompted the decision to strike at Anzio.

The strategic difference between Americans and British was the question of where to make the major effort in Europe. Across the Mediterranean and into the underbelly of the Continent? Or across the English Channel and into the northwestern reaches of the European land mass?

The British, tied for many years to Gibraltar, Malta, Egypt, and the oil-rich Near East, regarded the Mediterranean as the important area. Even before the United States became directly involved in the war, the British were fighting desperately on the sea and on the northern shore of Africa to retain control of the Mediterranean.

The Americans, acutely conscious of the demands of the war in the Pacific, wanted a quick decisive blow against the European partners, Germany and Italy. They saw victory as the result of a cross-Channel blow into northwest France and a subsequent campaign along the most direct route to Germany, the stronger of the two enemies. In the third month after Pearl Harbor, American planners were already working on an operation designed to get troops across the Channel and into major battle on the classic invasion routes into Germany.

The British did not entirely disagree with this concept. Their planners were also studying how best to land on the Continent and engage the German ground forces. But keenly aware of German strength and the difficulties of invading a hostile shore, they saw a cross-Channel attack as the climactic strike against a Germany debilitated by operations elsewhere. What they hoped was that sustained action on the Russian front and in the Mediterranean would bleed Germany and make her too weak to withstand a decisive cross-Channel operation. They wanted to be certain of success in the final blow of the war.

The crux of the argument was therefore a matter of timing. Yet both Allies could and did agree that the Americans should build up a great force of men and matériel in the United Kingdom for an eventual cross-Channel operation. The concentration of American troops and equipment in England was in process when the invasion of northwest Africa in November, 1942, drained off these resources to the Mediterranean.

In January, 1943, during the Casablanca conference, the Allies decided to invade Sicily that year—upon the completion of the North African campaign—in order to make the Mediterranean Sea safe for shipping, to divert German strength from Russia, and to increase pressure on Italy in the hope of forcing that nation out of the war. Because a shortage of landing craft and assault ships, heavy losses to German submarines, and strong German positions along the Atlantic coast of Europe ruled out a cross-Channel effort in 1943, the Allies decided to attack across the Channel in the spring of 1944. This would be the principal means of achieving victory in Europe. To that end they reinstated the American build-up in England.

The major reason why both Mediterranean and cross-Channel operations were not simultaneously possible was a lack of resources. The Allies did not have enough trained men, matériel, and supplies to carry out full-scale operations at the same time against the southern shore and the western coast of Europe. Though operations in the Mediterranean would draw off resources being collected in England, halting operations in the Mediterranean in favor of the build-up would permit the enemy to shift his defenses to meet the cross-Channel blow. Thus, to employ the military forces assembled in North Africa, the Allies chose Sicily for the next Mediterranean venture.

The trouble with Sicily—and at the same time its great advantage—was that it could be no more than a steppingstone to Europe. Beyond Sicily, where should the Allies go?

Americans who saw European strategy in terms of a cross-Channel attack looked to the western Mediterranean. They favored an invasion of southern France as a complementary and diversionary maneuver to the cross-Channel operation. This required prior steps into Sardinia and Corsica.

Inclined toward the Adriatic and Aegean areas of the Mediterranean, the British wished to support the guerrillas active in the Balkans, give incentive for Turkey to enter the war on the Allied side, and open a relatively short southern sea route to Russia for lend-lease supplies. To get into the eastern Mediterranean region, southern Italy was necessary for airfields and a logistical base.

Despite their divergent tendencies, one hope united both

Americans and British in the Mediterranean—hope that Italy, the weaker of the European Axis partners, could be forced out of the war. But here again the Allies differed. The British were willing to spend more than the Americans for Italian capitulation. The Americans were looking for some place to halt Mediterranean operations in order to make increased resources available in the Pacific and in the United Kingdom.

Still a third invasion route was possible, a campaign up the mainland of Italy, but this course was unattractive. If the Germans occupied Italy or stiffened Italian morale, they might force the Allies into a major and protracted campaign over difficult terrain. Since the Allied resources in the Mediterranean were inadequate to assure decisive success against determined opposition, the Allies would need additional troops and matériel. Otherwise, the most the Allies could do was to take the southern portion of the Italian boot.

A campaign confined to southern Italy would give the Allies air bases for bombing targets in the Balkans and southern Germany, but no decisive objectives beyond, possibly, a surrender of Italy, a surrendered Italy occupied by German troops. Whether this provided sufficient motivation for a difficult ground campaign was another question.

Meeting again in Washington in May, 1943, at the close of the North African campaign, the Allied leaders confirmed a cross-Channel invasion to be made on May 1, 1944, as the main operation in Europe. To insure success, they would make no further diversions of men, matériel, and supplies from the build-up in England to meet Mediterranean needs. Not only that—they would transfer seven Allied divisions from the Mediterranean area to the United Kingdom some time before the end of 1943.

They also scheduled the invasion of Sicily for July, 1943. But beyond Sicily they could still reach no agreement. The most they could do was to set forth two vague desiderata:

knock Italy out of the war and tie down the maximum number of German forces.

Increasing firmness for the cross-Channel attack contrasted with growing vagueness for Mediterranean operations, and this in part was due to the expanding American strength in the Allied coalition. Contributing more resources led inevitably to greater weight in determining strategy. As the coalition began to reflect to a larger extent an American point of view, Mediterranean strategy became diluted and imprecise. Exactly how to knock Italy out of the war and tie down the maximum number of Germans was not, perhaps could not be, outlined because of the strategic friction between the Allies. Exactly where to go beyond Sicily could not be resolved.

President Franklin D. Roosevelt and Prime Minister Winston S. Churchill together made the Allied strategic decisions. Helping them were their military advisers: the American Joint Chiefs of Staff—the officers at the head of the Army, Navy, and Air Force—and the British Chiefs of Staff—officers who held the same positions in their country. These officials in session together formed what was called the Combined Chiefs of Staff (CCS), and this group built the Allied strategy.

By the summer of 1943, Mr. Roosevelt was giving less attention to strategic matters than in the past. He had, for example, committed the United States to the North African invasion over the objections of his military staff, who had opposed what they considered a diversion of resources to the Mediterranean. As the strategic thinking swung back in 1943 toward the cross-Channel concept, Roosevelt became more interested in other problems—keeping China active in the war, shaping the postwar world. As the President came to depend ever more on the advice of his military staff, his principal military assistant, General George C. Marshall, U. S. Army Chief of Staff, emerged as the strongest American voice in the formulation of strategy.

From the beginning of the alliance, General Marshall had

espoused the direct thrust into northwest Europe as the quickest way to victory. To a large extent his insistence derived from his experience in World War I. Then, too, there had been controversy over the best way to defeat Germany. Some, called the "easterners," favored increasingly important operations in the Mediterranean and the Near East. Others, the "westerners," believed in seeking a showdown on the western front, in France. The latter had prevailed. Among them had been Pershing, and Marshall had become one of his closest associates. What Marshall feared most during much of World War II was that Mediterranean operations might absorb so many resources as to jeopardize a cross-Channel endeavor.

General Marshall's opposite number in the British camp was General Sir Alan Brooke, Chief of the Imperial General Staff. The exponent of what was sometimes called the indirect, or peripheral, strategy, he favored Mediterranean operations. Though he had the difficult task of serving a difficult master —Mr. Churchill was at one and the same time Brooke's great cross to bear and his great inspiration—Brooke managed to keep British strategic thought within the bounds of practicality and focused on the Mediterranean.

A Renaissance man somehow miraculously and marvelously misplaced into the twentieth century, Churchill had, it seemed, seen and done everything. Possessed of an unquenchable energy and curiosity, he left his personal imprint on all that he touched. Too active to play a passive role in any enterprise he was involved in, he harassed Brooke constantly, yet took his strategic advice, for he admired and respected Brooke's steadiness and military professionalism.

It would be Churchill, an "easterner" during World War I, who would engineer Anzio. And, significantly, Brooke would be absent when he did so. On this occasion, no one would exert the balance, the professional sagacity, the opposition that Churchill had come to expect from Brooke. An unfettered Churchill would beguile himself and others by a dazzling vision. He was, as he said, "passionately" interested in Rome.

Charged with executing Roosevelt's and Churchill's instructions was General Dwight D. Eisenhower. Supreme Commander of the Allied Force in North Africa, he had gained his reputation as the man who had made coalition warfare work smoothly. Differences are bound to develop between national forces engaged in a common pursuit, but in Eisenhower's command, friction had been reduced to a minimum.

Affable and inclined to be easy-going, Eisenhower had chosen a perfect foil as his chief of staff, Major General Walter Bedell Smith, who was tough and on the brusque side. Together they made an excellent team.

Under Eisenhower were ground, naval, and air forces of the United States, the British Commonwealth of Nations, and the Free French. Not only was Eisenhower responsible for joint operations—that is, synchronizing the ground, naval, and air forces; but he was also charged with combined operations —that is, using the forces of the different nations in a fair and judicious manner, balancing the contributions and sacrifices of each national participant according to his resources, special aptitudes, and traditional interests.

Influenced to a great extent by British command practice, Eisenhower made important decisions usually only after consulting with his subordinate commanders. He called frequent conferences and listened carefully to what his principal advisers had to say. But in the end he conformed to the American doctrine of single command responsibility. The decisions were his alone.

General Eisenhower's principal subordinate commanders were British officers who, in each case, commanded combined Anglo-American forces and who, together with General Smith, comprised Eisenhower's closest official circle. Air Chief Marshal Sir Arthur Tedder commanded the Allied air forces. Admiral Sir Andrew B. Cunningham directed Allied naval operations. General Sir Harold R. L. G. Alexander, Eisenhower's deputy commander-in-chief, also commanded the ground forces, and he would have much to do with Anzio.

One of those fortunate persons who are born with all the advantages, General Alexander came from a distinguished family and was endowed with intelligence, good looks, and charm. Equally at ease in evening clothes and riding breeches, he seemed to go through life without care, worry, or even effort. Everything came easy to him, and his imperturbable coolness made him appear unconcerned even in the most heated moments of crisis. He was, as Brooke said, "ever completely composed." And he never had "the slightest doubt that all would come out right in the end."

A division commander during the 1940 campaign in France, Alexander proved his fitness for high command by his sound judgment and balance. One of the last to leave the beleaguered beachhead at Dunkirk, he had later been assigned to Cairo, Egypt, to take over from Auchinleck at a time when British fortunes in World War II were at their lowest ebb. As the commander responsible for co-ordinating the forces that gained the resounding victory at El Alamein, he won his reputation.

General Alexander's introduction to American troops was not a happy occasion. The American ground forces, their commanders and staffs, were new to combat in North Africa. Largely because they lacked experience, they suffered a serious setback at Kasserine Pass. On this Alexander judged them, and, as a result, he tended to favor the British veterans who had proved their combat proficiency. Only after the performance of the Seventh U. S. Army under George S. Patton, Jr., in Sicily changed Alexander's mind did he demonstrate his ability to work on an Allied rather than a national basis. He soon made it quite apparent that he could be equitable in the assignments he made and the expectations he held. Though some American commanders continued to resent Alexander, Eisenhower termed him "broad-gauged."

As Mediterranean prospects were debated in the summer of 1943, the British Chiefs of Staff began to judge a campaign on the Italian mainland, despite the potential difficulties, far more beneficial than an invasion of Sardinia and Corsica.

The Americans, in contrast, remained disturbed over the possibility of drifting into a major land campaign that might have an unfavorable effect on a cross-Channel invasion. They preferred Sardinia and Corsica, which would require fewer resources and were on the road to southern France.

No decision was reached until after the invasion of Sicily in July, 1943, when the relative ease of the landings and comparatively light losses in men and matériel showed clearly how far Italian combat power had declined.

For British planners in London, the time seemed right to be bold and to assume great risks. The Allies should, they thought, invade the Italian mainland as the means for driving Italy out of the war. The most promising target on the mainland was Naples, obviously the first step in a march to Rome.

American planners in Washington hesitated to endorse a Naples operation, which might lead to a long and indecisive peninsular campaign probably requiring additional resources that would affect the build-up in England. They objected on the ground that a Naples landing would interfere with the global strategy projected earlier that year at Casablanca and at Washington.

British planners nevertheless went ahead with studies and plans. Because capture of Naples would be a serious blow to the Axis and capture of Rome a decisive *coup*, a Naples invasion would no doubt prompt Italian capitulation. Because Italian surrender would probably compel the Germans to extricate their forces from southern Italy, the Allies could come quickly into possession of airfields and a base from which to threaten the Balkans and Greece as well as southern France.

The CCS agreed. But how much, in terms of resources, should be expended?

British strategists wished to retain as many resources in the Mediterranean as possible. They thought it a mistake to deprive Eisenhower of anything he might need for a successful invasion of Italy and a subsequent advance. There was no changing the Americans on the prior decision to move seven divisions out of the Mediterranean, but why should not other resources destined for England, India, and the Pacific stay in the theater until Eisenhower determined what he needed?

The Americans demurred. Operations projected in Burma, primarily to assist China, required the release of some amphibious craft from the Mediterranean. But more important was the threat to the cross-Channel build-up. If sufficient resources were available in the theater to seize Sardinia, as had already been decided, why did Eisenhower need more for Naples?

The CCS compromised. They instructed Eisenhower to invade Naples with the resources he already had. He would get no additional forces for an Italian campaign.

A dramatic event occurring in Rome on July 25 underscored the decision. King Victor Emmanuel removed Benito Mussolini from power and installed Marshal Pietro Badoglio as head of a new government. Though Badoglio immediately announced that Italy would continue in the war, the elimination of Italy suddenly seemed much closer at hand.

In Washington the military leaders now considered an increase of Eisenhower's resources altogether unnecessary. A swift descent on Naples and a short campaign in Italy seemed possible and even likely.

Yet, when they met again in August, 1943, at Quebec, the Allied leaders continued to argue about strategy. Though they accepted an outline plan prepared that summer for a cross-

Channel attack—a plan with the code name of OVERLORD —they debated their disparate views. The British, essentially opportunistic, wanted to keep the timing of OVERLORD indefinite. The Americans, committed wholeheartedly to a cross-Channel invasion, wished a definite target date.

In the end the Americans had their way. Not only on OVERLORD, but also on an invasion of southern France. Timed to coincide with OVERLORD, a complementary and diversionary invasion of southern France received priority over other Mediterranean operations. In case of a conflict over resources, the projected Italian campaign would suffer, for Eisenhower was to invade southern France with the resources he had available in the Mediterranean.

The assumption was that the Allied forces would certainly have advanced well beyond Naples and Rome by the spring of 1944, the time of the cross-Channel attack. Holding a line somewhere in northern Italy, possibly in the vicinity of Pisa and Rimini, the Allies would be tieing down sizable German forces. They would also be in position to divert a good part of their resources to southern France in order to assist the cross-Channel venture.

What the Allied leaders failed to take sufficiently into account was the extent and the strength of the defensive effort that was possible in the rugged Italian terrain.

On the day that Italy surrendered, September 3, 1943, General Sir Bernard L. Montgomery's British Eighth Army crossed the Strait of Messina from Sicily and landed in the toe of Italy against virtually no opposition.

On September 9, a day after the Italian surrender was announced to the world, and incidentally to the Germans, Allied warships ferried a British division for a landing on the Italian heel against absolutely no opposition.

On the same day, Lieutenant General Mark W. Clark's Fifth U. S. Army—two British divisions of the X Corps and a

single American division in the VI Corps—battled ashore at
Salerno. The Allies met opposition at the water's edge, and a
raging battle ensued.

Everyone on the Allied side had expected Salerno to be
risky. In large part an invasion is a race between opponents,
each of whom is trying to rush more troops than the other to
the battlefield. The invaders coming by sea must build up their
beachhead—that is, the initial piece of ground they seize—
more quickly than the enemy can reinforce those who defend
the ground. If enough ships are available, and if airplanes are
bombing and strafing the enemy's roads and railways and
thereby interfering with his movements, the invader can make
his beachhead so strong that he cannot be dislodged. But if
the defender can throw a strong force against the invaders
before the latter are securely ashore, the invasion is likely to
end in tragedy and failure. At Salerno the Allies did not have
enough vessels to get enough men ashore ahead of the reinforcements the Germans were rushing to the threatened spot.
Nor could they furnish sufficient aircraft—because of the distance to Salerno from the airfields in Sicily—to disrupt German movements to the battlefield.

Clark's forces came ashore on one of the few open pieces
of ground in southern Italy, on a plain hemmed in by mountains. The effect was like fighting in an amphitheater under
the eyes of the Germans who sat in the stands and were able
to send their spectators into the battle at vital moments of the
conflict.

On the fifth day of the invasion, the Germans came close
to driving the Allies off their beaches. Such words as "unfavorable," "tense," and "critical" crept into the Allied reports from
the beachhead. The crisis then passed, and the Germans began
to withdraw up the Italian peninsula.

Despite the victory, the Salerno landing left the Allies a
legacy that hung like a dark cloud over the entire Italian campaign. Anzio would suffer from it.

When the Germans began to withdraw from Salerno, they followed a course of action predetermined by their strategic thinking. Their decision to retire up the peninsula, from their point of view, was logical.

The Italian surrender had not come as a complete surprise to Hitler. He had distrusted his Italian ally for some time. Yet uncertainty over Italy's intentions complicated his preparations for defending Italy and the Mediterranean area, for he had to be concerned not only with Allied intentions but also with Italian aims.

In the summer of 1942, Hitler had envisioned his armored columns advancing through North Africa and the Caucasus to a juncture somewhere in the Near East, the most gigantic pincer movement in history. By mid-1943, deprived of the strategic initiative and forced on the defensive everywhere, he faced the problem of meeting Allied operations in the Mediterranean without being able to rely on Italy for a fair share of the defense.

The staggering losses he had suffered at Stalingrad, his loss of superiority in air power, the increasing vulnerability of his lines of communication to bombardment added to his problems.

With no positive plan for victory beyond an *Endsieg*, a final triumph based on irrational hope and mystic faith, Hitler, though holding supreme economic, political, and military power, had no single strategic plan embracing all theaters of operation. He had no unified command or joint staff directing the entire national war effort. Nor did he consider it desirable to keep his military associates informed of his political goals.

Convinced upon Mussolini's deposition from power that Italy would not continue in the war much longer, Hitler was nevertheless reluctant to take the first step toward an open break or to give the Italians an excuse to defect. For if the Italian government could not bring itself to accept the Allied unconditional surrender, Italy might perhaps remain in the war.

In the event of Italian defection, Hitler had several strategic alternatives: defend all of Italy and the Balkans, surrender all Italian territory, or defend Italy along some geographic line to prevent loss of the rich agricultural and industrial resources of the Po valley.

Hitler never seriously considered evacuating all of Italy. Allied air bases in northern Italy would be too close to south and central Germany, and Allied amphibious operations against southern France and Yugoslavia too easy to launch. Withdrawal to the Alps might give Hungary and other Balkan satellites the idea that they could disengage from the war; it might also have an adverse effect on Turkish neutrality.

Though Hitler's first idea was to occupy and defend all of Italy, he soon concluded that he could retain only part of the country somewhere in the north. For he believed, as he told his closest military associates, "we cannot hold the entire peninsula without the Italian army." He instructed Field Marshal Erwin Rommel to activate an army group headquarters at Munich for the purpose of occupying northern Italy in case of Italian defection and defending Italy in the north in case of Allied invasion.

Hitler figured that the Allies would invade the Italian mainland only after reaching agreement with Italy and in order to capitalize on Italian surrender. What he feared most in this case was the isolation of German forces in southern Italy. If the Allies staged an amphibious operation against northern Italy while defecting Italian troops blocked the Alpine and Apennine passes, or if the Allies landed near Rome while Italian divisions blocked German forces south of the capital, the Germans would lose a considerable number of troops.

Yet a campaign limited to the Italian peninsula, Hitler believed, was impractical for the Allies. The terrain was too advantageous for defense. More feasible, it seemed to Hitler, were Sardinia as a prelude to further operations against northern Italy or southern France, and the heel, particularly because of the air bases at Foggia, as the introduction to an Allied advance into the Balkans.

Because of the political, economic, and military factors involved, Hitler regarded the Balkans, not Italy, as the Allied strategic goal. The Ljubljana Gap was a classic invasion route into central Europe. Allied invasion of southeast Europe would enable the western Allies and Russia to join in a co-ordinated strategy. The presence of western troops would check Russian ambitions in that area, a point Hitler thought to be of particular concern to the British.

In Italy, Hitler had no idea of defending anywhere south of Rome. He instructed Rommel to occupy all the important mountain passes, roads, and railways in northern Italy; disarm the Italian army units; and make the Apennine passes secure. Meanwhile, the forces in southern Italy were to withdraw to the north, disarming the Italian army and crushing opposition as they went. When the troops in northern Italy "became operationally connected with those in southern Italy," as Hitler put it, Rommel was to assume command over all the German forces in the Italian peninsula.

In southern Italy an air force officer, Field Marshal Albert Kesselring, commanded the German forces. A natural optimist and political idealist, with distinct Italophile views, Kesselring was convinced that Italy would continue in the war. Working closely with the Italian High Command, he disliked to hear talk of Hitler's distrust of the Italians. He found rumors of evacuating Italy even worse. He objected strongly to Rommel's uncomplimentary remarks about Italian soldiers. And he resented the fact that his own influence with Hitler seemed to be declining as Rommel's increased. Shocked by Mussolini's fall from power, Kesselring accepted in good faith Badoglio's declarations of continuing the war effort. Believing wholeheartedly that all of Italy could and should be defended, Kesselring saw no danger to his forces, no menace to his lines of communication, and little reason to withdraw from the south.

What he needed, he felt, was reinforcement so that he could properly defend the toe and the heel.

Despite repeated requests for more troops, Kesselring received only the Tenth Army headquarters. The Tenth Army commander, General Heinrich von Vietinghoff *genannt* Scheel, had orders not to help Kesselring hold southern Italy indefinitely but to insure the safe withdrawal of German forces from southern Italy to the Rome area in case of Italian defection. But Vietinghoff was to make no premature retrograde movements. The Italian toe was to be evacuated only under Allied pressure, the Naples–Salerno area held only to assure the safe retirement of the troops from the toe.

Withdrawal to the Rome area was to be the first step toward a front north of Rome. In northern Italy, behind a strong defensive line, Hitler would clear Italy of Italian troops and pacify the civilians. He would then send three or four divisions to the Balkans, which he considered "vulnerable to an Anglo-Saxon attack."

When the British crossed the Strait of Messina, Kesselring, in accordance with Hitler's plans, ordered the two German divisions in the toe to fight a delaying action while withdrawing to the north. Upon news of the Italian surrender, German units began at once to disarm the Italian army and take over their coastal defenses. When the Allied invasion force arrived at Salerno, the Germans were preparing to oppose the landings. Since the two divisions withdrawing from the toe were still below Salerno, Kesselring and Vietinghoff, in order to protect the retrograde movement of these divisions, made what they called a "ruthless concentration of all forces at Salerno."

When the last of the German troops withdrawing from the toe arrived at Salerno, Kesselring broke off the engagement. The Germans moved up the Italian boot toward Rome and eventual juncture with the forces under Rommel.

Kesselring was satisfied with the outcome of the battle.

No German troops had been trapped. The Allies had been denied quick access to Naples. And the Germans had created a continuous front across the Italian peninsula, from the Tyrrhenian Sea to the Adriatic.

"Success has been ours," Vietinghoff proclaimed. "Once again German soldiers have proved their superiority over the enemy."

"The Germans," Alexander admitted, "may claim with some justification to have won if not a victory at least an important success over us."

Since the German strategic planning projected a withdrawal from southern Italy regardless of the outcome of the battle at Salerno, the Germans did not bring additional strength from the north, from Rommel's command, though this might well have turned the balance. Though the Germans would have liked to repel the invasion for political as well as for military reasons, though total victory at Salerno would no doubt have changed the strategic thinking, the German resistance at Salerno was postulated on the less decisive motive of assuring withdrawal.

The result of the battle at Salerno might well have been different had the Germans, from the outset, been differently inclined. And this thought was not lost on the Allied commanders. They had had a close call.

THE STALEMATE

2   SOON AFTER Salerno, as the Fifth U. S. Army advanced up the west coast to Naples (for its port) and the British Eighth Army moved up the east coast to Foggia (for its airfields), both armies operating under Alexander's control, the question of where to go in the peninsula of Italy came under debate. Should the Allies continue up the mainland? If so, how far?

The answers depended on several related questions: How could the Allied forces in the Mediterranean best assist the cross-Channel attack? By threatening the Germans in the Balkans? Or by menacing southern France? What could be expected from the resources allotted to the theater? Should Eisenhower try to secure more men and matériel from the CCS?

The difficulty in finding answers lay in the CCS directive that governed the campaign. The order to tie down the Germans was so vague as to be virtually indefinable. How contain the maximum number of German forces? In the absence of geographical objectives, an absence due to Anglo-American differences on the strategic conduct of the war, the Italian campaign became a great holding attack. Exactly who was holding whom was never quite clear. Still, in order to give meaning to field operations, objectives were necessary, goals toward which the troops could look and fight.

A campaign up the entire length of the Italian peninsula required more resources than a campaign designed to secure, say, Rome. And in discussing resources, those who directed the campaign sought to secure as many troops, as much equipment and supplies as possible, not only to make the campaign easier but also because one's own tasks normally assume great importance and because it is natural to build empires.

Eisenhower's planners expected the Germans to withdraw to the Alps or to a line in northern Italy, trying to delay the Allies as they retired. But if the Germans turned and fought, was the occupation of northern Italy worth while? Beyond Naples, Rome was the obvious next objective. What then? Why go farther? The heel of Italy gave the Allies control of the south Adriatic and Ionian Seas. Air and naval forces operating from the heel could hamper the movement of German supplies to Greece and Albania, support the partisans in Yugoslavia, and threaten the Balkans sufficiently to contain German forces there. Similarly, possession of Sardinia and Corsica—the Germans evacuated the islands after Salerno— gave the Allies control of the Tyrrhenian Sea and provided verisimilitude to the threat of a landing in southern France. Ten French divisions were expected to be ready in North Africa for operations early in 1944, and these troops would comprise a real danger to the Germans. Thus, the Allies could contain the maximum number of Germans if they occupied no more than southern Italy as far north as Rome and the islands of Sardinia and Corsica.

That was all that American planners in Washington were interested in—Naples, Rome, air bases as far north as possible, and "unremitting pressure" against the Germans as prelude to an invasion of southern France. They saw no reason to go all the way up the Italian peninsula.

If the Germans reinforced their troops in Italy, Eisenhower believed, a firm grasp on Naples would be a respectable accomplishment. Whether the available Allied forces could go farther north depended entirely on how much strength the Germans put into Italy. Yet it was impractical, he thought, to have an Allied army in central Italy, a German army in northern Italy, and a no-man's land between. Either the Allies would have to drive the Germans out of Italy entirely or fight hard to prevent their own ejection. Without increased resources, Eisenhower warned the CCS, the Allies faced severe and bitter fighting. A firm hold on Naples might be the extent of what he could accomplish. Or, the Allies would have to fight their way "slowly and painfully" up the peninsula.

The CCS had their eyes fixed elsewhere. They instructed Eisenhower to plan an invasion of southern France and be ready to execute it at some time during or after the Italian campaign. Though the time was unspecified, an invasion of southern France was to be simultaneous with OVERLORD. The CCS, therefore, expected the Italian campaign to be at least near completion by the spring of 1944. By then, they thought, the Allies would surely have forced the Germans back to the Alps.

Eisenhower was not so sure. German strength, he estimated, would probably force the Allies into a methodical advance up the leg of Italy during the winter months. Was a methodical advance worth the effort? Would battle elsewhere than on the inhospitable Italian terrain give quicker results with less expenditures? The conquest of Italy, he told Marshall, was a highly debatable proposition.

On the other hand, Eisenhower noted, perhaps the Germans would be too nervous to stand for a real battle south of Rome. They were heading, he thought, for a line near Cassino, not to create a final defensive position but to cover Rome and insure their own retrograde movements. They had evacuated Sardinia and Corsica, and this would indicate their intention to make a fairly rapid withdrawal from southern and central

Italy. The Germans, Eisenhower estimated, might well pull back to the Pisa–Rimini line, far above Rome.

By the end of the first week in October, General Eisenhower's optimism had vanished. The Germans, it now appeared, were bringing down divisions from northern Italy to reinforce the troops fighting in the south. This was no withdrawal. "Clearly," Eisenhower informed the CCS, "there will be very hard and bitter fighting before we can hope to reach Rome."

Was it possible to remain along a line in southern Italy? Eisenhower thought not. A line well north of Rome was needed to protect Naples and Foggia and make feasible an invasion of southern France.

Furthermore, nothing would help OVERLORD as much, Eisenhower and his senior commanders believed, as the early establishment of Allied forces in northern Italy. Since the Germans seemed to have determined to resist in southern Italy, could Eisenhower have additional resources for the difficult campaign bound to take place? Could Eisenhower have certain resources necessary to carry out small amphibious operations in the enemy rear to hasten the advance up the peninsula?

No, said the CCS. There would be no increase in the Mediterranean resources.

Whether the Allies had enough troops, equipment, and supplies to drive to northern Italy against strong German opposition was a moot question. But there was no alternative except to try.

Withdrawing slowly from Salerno, Kesselring looked for good natural defensive lines in southern Italy on which to delay the Allies. A slow retirement would not only help conserve his forces but would also defer the need to pass his forces and his command over to Rommel in northern Italy.

While searching for delaying positions, Kesselring was struck by the natural strength of the ground at Cassino, 70 miles south of Rome. A line through the mountains around Cassino and across the Italian peninsula offered the opportunity for more than temporary defense. If he could hold off the Allies long enough during the fall of 1943 to fortify a line at Cassino, he might be able to go over on the defensive altogether. That is, if he could persuade Hitler to change his mind on the strategy to be followed in Italy.

To this end, Kesselring bent his efforts. So skillfully did he fall back that he reduced the Allied advance to a painful crawl.

Kesselring's unexpected success in retarding Allied progress raised his stock in Hitler's eyes. After the Allies failed to make the landings Hitler anticipated near Rome, Kesselring's advocacy of a defense of Italy south of Rome gained considerable force.

Kesselring pointed out that a prolonged defense in southern Italy would delay a Balkan invasion. Allied bombers operating from Foggia rather than from bases in the north would be farther from the Po valley and Germany, their bombings therefore less effective. Rome in German hands had obvious political advantages. And fewer soldiers would be needed to hold at the Cassino line, the narrowest part of the peninsula, than anywhere else in Italy.

Rommel sponsored an opposite viewpoint. A defense in southern Italy, he maintained, could be too easily outflanked by Allied amphibious operations.

Kesselring's optimism, earlier a source of irritation, began to impress Hitler favorably. Rommel, in contrast, appeared pessimistic, even defeatist. Late in September, therefore, Hitler told Kesselring to continue his slow withdrawal to the north but to hold the Cassino line "for a longer period of time."

Soon afterwards, early in October, Hitler told Kesselring to defend the Cassino line in strength. Hitler was not entirely convinced that Kesselring could halt the Allies for six to nine months as Kesselring had estimated—Kesselring, after all, was not an army commander but an air force general—yet Hitler was going to give Kesselring his opportunity. He ordered Rommel to send Kesselring two infantry divisions and some artillery from northern Italy.

Hitler thus hoped to hold on to Rome and tie down the Allies in a battle of attrition to prevent them from invading the Balkans. But Hitler also had another reason. As he told Marshal Rodolfo Graziani, chief of the fascist army of Mussolini's new government formed in the north: "The defense of the [Cassino] line is of decisive importance to the continuance of a joint [Italo-German] struggle."

In reality, Hitler had not definitely made up his mind whether or not to make a stand south of Rome. He watched the fighting. For another month he consulted with Rommel, who remained pessimistic and negative, and with Kesselring, ever buoyant and optimistic.

Finally, on November 6, Hitler made his decision. He transferred Rommel to France on a special assignment to strengthen the Atlantic Wall in anticipation of an Allied invasion of northwest Europe. He appointed Kesselring supreme commander of the German troops in Italy. To Kesselring he specified that the Cassino line was to "mark the end of withdrawals."

Though neither side knew of the other's action in this respect, the Allies were coming to their decision at this time to execute an amphibious assault on the beaches of Anzio.

Kesselring—having won his strategic controversy with Rommel and enjoying firm backing from Hitler—prepared to defend the approaches to Rome with vigor. He would do his utmost to be worthy of his Fuehrer's confidence.

Hitler's decision had some elements of a gamble. By holding in southern Italy and maintaining long lines of communication, he made his troops vulnerable to amphibious attack and his supply lines vulnerable to air attack. Yet his primary motive was the hope of preventing an Allied invasion of the Balkans.

Though the Allies had no real intention of making a move of this sort, rapid conquest of southern and central Italy might possibly have tempted them into the venture. Instead, the effect of Hitler's decision was to make the road to Rome a long, hard trek, with adverse reverberations on the Allied troops, on Germany's allies in southern Europe, and on the neutral nations, especially Turkey.

The Germans could fight effectively only on the ground, for in air and naval power they were sadly deficient. The Italian fleet of five battleships and nine cruisers had been a substantial Axis force in the Mediterranean, but when these capital ships and other lesser vessels sailed into Allied harbors in September, 1943, in conformance with the terms of the Italian surrender, the Germans were left with only a few small gunboats and auxiliary craft. These naval elements rarely ventured from the protected harbors of northern Italy. Except for an occasional submarine that slipped through the Strait of Gibraltar, the German naval force was too insignificant and weak for even a demonstration against the Allied sea power that consisted of aircraft carriers, battleships, cruisers, destroyers, and a host of supporting vessels.

In the air the Second German Air Force (*Luftflotte 2*) could make a better showing. There were about 2,000 German and Italian planes of all kinds in the Mediterranean area. About 500 of the Italian craft were obsolete and of little value. The rest compared well with their Allied counterparts. Yet no more than 50 per cent were available for operations at any one time because of serious shortages of gasoline, spare parts, and trained pilots and crews.

By the end of 1943 the Germans would have about 550 operational aircraft in Italy, southern France, and the Balkans. Almost all the big bombers would by then have been withdrawn from Italian fields to prevent their destruction on the ground by Allied air attack. The only long-range craft available for heavy bombardments in Italy would be about 50 JU-88's based in Greece and Crete, and approximately 60 JU-88's, He-111's, and Do-217's in southern France. Most of the fighters—about 230 Me-109's and FW-190's—would still be in Italy, with about one-third of them on fields around Rome. But the German air force would make its presence felt.

A new weapon increased the effectiveness of German air warfare. This was the "glider" bomb, directed from plane to target by radio control or by a homing device. Fitted with wings and rocket-assisted, this armor-piercing bomb had low velocity and a delayed fuze, was 19 inches in diameter, and weighed about 2,500 pounds. The bomb was effective against ships, as was demonstrated at Salerno and as would again become apparent at Anzio.

In comparison with the diminishing strength of the German air force, the Allies had 2,600 aircraft in the Mediterranean, most of them moving in the latter months of 1943 from North African airfields to bases in Italy, Sardinia, and Corsica. In contrast with the low ratio of serviceable German craft, Allied planes were considered 75 per cent available at all times. The heavy bombers (B-17 Flying Fortresses, B-24 Liberators) designed to attack strategic targets deep in the enemy rear, the medium bombers (B-25 Mitchells, B-26 Marauders, and Wellingtons) to strike targets 50 to 100 miles or more behind the enemy front, the light bombers (A-20 Bostons, DAF Baltimores) to destroy installations and facilities closer to the front, the fighter-bombers (A-36 Invaders and Mosquitoes) to give direct support to the ground troops, and the fighter planes (P-38 Lightnings, P-40 Hawks, P-47 Thunderbolts, P-51 Mustangs, Spitfires, and Hurricanes) to escort bombers and to intercept and attack enemy craft—these comprised an impressively balanced force of air power.

Against this Allied strength the Germans could do no more than make sneak attacks and raids. Rarely could they support their own ground troops.

It was on the ground that the Germans could meet the Allies with more than a show of equality. German divisions, whether infantry, panzer grenadier, paratroop, or panzer, were much alike, differing only in the proportions of infantrymen, tanks, artillery, and vehicles. A German division numbered between 10,000 and 17,000 men according to its type, with 6 battalions of infantry organized into 2 or 3 regiments, with 1 or 2 tank battalions, 1 to 3 battalions of artillery, and the usual complements of engineer, signal, and supporting troops.

American and British divisions were somewhat heavier, numbering about 17,000 men. The U. S. infantry division had 3 infantry regiments, each with 3 battalions of infantry; 3 battalions of light artillery (105-mm. howitzers); 1 battalion of medium artillery (155-mm. howitzers); an attached tank battalion and an attached tank destroyer battalion; plus reconnaissance, support, and service elements. The British division usually had 2 infantry brigades, each with 3 rifle battalions; 1 tank brigade of 3 tank battalions; much the same artillery organization (24- and 25-pounders, 4.5-inch guns, and 5.5-inch howitzers); plus the usual supporting units.

German and Allied weapons were similar, the standard infantry arms—rifles, machine guns, and mortars—being approximately equal in effectiveness, American tank destroyers and German assault guns about the same, the bazooka rocket launcher much like the *panzerfaust*.

Three German weapons were superior. The 88-mm. high-velocity dual-purpose antiaircraft and antitank piece was probably the outstanding artillery weapon of World War II. The machine pistol, distributed liberally among infantrymen and called by the Americans the burp gun, was particularly effective for close-in fighting. And the multiple-barrel 150-mm. mortar mounted on wheels and fired electrically, the *nebelwerfer* called the "screaming meemies," though available in Italy only in small quantities, delivered a frightening, demoralizing noise along with its destructive effect.

Offsetting these advantages were two factors on the Allied side: the overwhelming superiority of artillery ammunition supplies and the wealth of wheeled and tracked vehicles and equipment. Whereas the Germans had always to watch their ammunition expenditures carefully, the Allies, and particularly the Americans, were comparatively wasteful; the Allies preferred to saturate their targets. Developed in Italy to the point of perfection was the technique of massing numerous battalions of artillery, sometimes as many as 40 at one time, on a given target, all the shells calculated to descend on the target simultaneously. Called the "serenade," time on target fire—the "TOT" as it was later termed—was employed with great effect. Tiny liaison airplanes, slow-flying single-engine L-4 Piper Cubs sometimes called "Grasshoppers," were normal adjuncts of American artillery, for observers riding over the German lines could spot targets and direct artillery fire with marvelous accuracy. The appearance of a single Grasshopper was sometimes enough to silence the German artillery within sight, for by firing their guns the Germans gave away their hidden positions and made them vulnerable to Allied counter-battery shoots.

In the number of jeeps, trucks, and earth-moving machinery, and in the technique of bridge-building, the Allies were far superior to the Germans, who depended on horse-drawn transport and, to a much greater extent than the Allies, on the labor of manpower. The 2½-ton American truck, much better than the 2-ton British lorry in power, capacity, and serviceability, was the workhorse of the war. The engineer bulldozer was invaluable.

The virtual absence of air support and the comparative deficiencies in matériel handicapped the German soldier, but at the same time challenged his ingenuity and forced him to develop the art of ground warfare to a high measure of efficiency. A fighter who was ruthless, clever, and well-trained, the German soldier in Italy was usually a veteran. His unit

was generally experienced, his leadership thoroughly professional. The army reflected the homogeneity of the German
nation and the strong sense of discipline among the German
people. Unity and cohesiveness imparted additional strength.
When that strength was employed defensively in the advantageous terrain of southern Italy, the Germans proved to be
a formidable foe.

Alexander could well understand the German decision to
stand and fight. The Germans, he judged, had recovered from
the shock of the Italian surrender. The country was quiet.
With better knowledge of Allied strength, the Germans estimated they had as many, if not more, ground troops than the
Allies. The terrain south of Rome was admirably suited for
defensive warfare. Autumn and winter weather would hamper
Allied offensive operations and curtail Allied air power. Kesselring's forces had been in continuous retreat since November,
1942; for almost a year, from just short of Alexandria, Egypt,
to just north of Naples. In the view of the Allied commander,
it was time for the Germans to stop, to retain as much of Italy
as possible for troop morale and political reasons. And it was
desirable to give a certain semblance of authority to the recently created Republican Fascist government under Mussolini by letting it have as much territory as possible to gov-
ern under German supervision.

Though the Allies encountered progressively stronger
resistance in Italy, their objective remained Rome. Churchill
had made evident on numerous occasions his "very strong desire" for the capital city. "Nothing less than Rome," he said,
"could satisfy the requirements of this year's campaign." Allied leaders at Quebec in September echoed this thought.
Though they "appreciated that our progress in Italy is likely
to be slow," they stressed "the importance of securing the
Rome aerodromes." Even General Marshall, who was luke-
warm on the advantages of continuing the Italian campaign,

agreed that the Allies ought to seize Rome as quickly as possible. And Eisenhower, who had thought of moving his headquarters from Algiers to Naples, decided to wait until he could "make the jump straight into Rome."

But German success in retarding the Allied advance caused the Allies to wonder whether tieing down the Germans and capturing Rome might be mutually incompatible.

In one sense, the German defense in southern Italy played into Allied hands, for it permitted the Allies to carry out the CCS directive. By allowing themselves to be contained in Italy, the Germans had removed not only the possibility of but also the necessity for an Allied campaign in the Balkans to divert the Germans from the western shore of France. For Italy was far enough away to permit the Italian campaign to be an effective diversion for the cross-Channel attack.

Yet the Germans, by their implacable defense, were denying the Allies access to Rome, the single decisive objective on the field of battle. During the month of October the Fifth U. S. Army advanced hardly at all above the Volturno River, and Rome remained more than one hundred long miles away, across convulsed and tangled mountains.

For the Allies, one thing was certain. They could not let the Germans rest. They could not give the Germans time to construct fortifications in Italy so strong as to tie down the Allies and at the same time make possible a transfer of their own troops to Russia or to France. The Allies had to keep the Germans occupied until spring at the earliest. And this meant the necessity of continuing the attack.

Continuing to attack in Italy meant breaching a series of strong positions anchored on favorable terrain features. It meant a winter campaign in increasingly unfavorable weather. It meant fighting on ground that inhibited maneuver and denied the effective use of Allied artillery and tanks.

Could the Allies exert enough pressure to throw the Germans off balance? Probably not. The Allied ground troops were no longer in first-rate condition. Some units already were badly in need of rest. Not only the terrain but slender resources hampered the Allies.

Now the problems the Allies had foreseen all along became real and upsetting. Limited by the mountains to frontal attack, the Allies could maneuver only by making seaborne hooks, by enveloping the enemy positions with amphibious "end runs." Yet this kind of operation was not easy. Only about a division could be spared from the main front for an amphibious landing. And since the Germans were capable of a rapid build-up, a single division would obviously fail unless the forces on the main front could link up with the beachhead within at least forty-eight hours. Thus, a landing could not be too far in advance of the front.

To use more than one division in a landing was impractical, for the Allies lacked the ships to transport so large a force. Unless, of course, they curtailed other supply operations, and this was undesirable. But even an assault force of two divisions could not maintain itself for long far away from the main front.

What did seem possible to speed progress in Italy was to launch small end runs closely tied in with the main forces. But because of the distance of the Allies from Rome, end runs promised no quick or decisive victory.

From the first, Eisenhower had recognized the necessity for amphibious turning movements and the difficulty of executing them. When the CCS remarked that Alexander was not showing much initiative and imagination in his operations, Eisenhower explained why. "If we landed a small force," he wrote, "it would be quickly eliminated, while a force large enough to sustain itself cannot possibly be mounted for a very considerable period." A small force of Commandos or Rangers, Eisenhower added, "would not last twenty-four hours because there is no place on the west coast where a full enemy division cannot be concentrated against us in twelve hours."

An amphibious attack was the only way to circumvent a slow and costly battle in Italy, but how and where to launch it remained a question. "The lack of proper shipping, difficult terrain, poor road net together with possible isolation of the force," a division commander noted in his diary, "make the project most difficult." A special planning staff investigating all possible amphibious opportunities could come up with no clear-cut recommendation because of the shortage of available troops and landing craft, the absence of suitable beaches, and the long distance of the Fifth Army from Rome.

As autumn turned into winter and the Germans continued to deny quick access to Rome, the bitterly fought campaign in southern Italy approached a stalemate. The fact now became indisputable: the only way to transform the static warfare into a war of movement was to launch a surprise amphibious landing behind the enemy lines. Since the Allies could anticipate no sudden surge forward to get the front closer to Rome, they turned their attention to securing additional ships to transport a larger force in a landing. A larger assault force had a better chance of withstanding German countermeasures for the longer time it would have to await link-up with the main front forces.

But obtaining more ships was virtually impossible. Priority for the Mediterranean theater in the developing global strategy was constantly slipping, and Eisenhower was to lose not only some of his veteran divisions but most of his amphibious equipment, the bulk scheduled to go to England for the eventual cross-Channel operation. Eventually he was to release to other theaters more than three-quarters of his landing ships and two-thirds of his landing craft. "All our operations," Eisenhower complained, "are strictly regulated by the availability of ships and landing craft," and he alluded often to this "constantly annoying and limiting factor."

If the landing ships and craft were returned as scheduled, only enough would remain in the theater for no more than a regimental-size amphibious attack. On the other hand, if the theater could keep most of the vessels until mid-December, a division-size assault might be possible. If the theater could hold on to the ships until early January, and if supply operations requiring vessels were severely curtailed, a landing in two-division strength might possibly be executed.

With these thoughts in mind, General Eisenhower and his principal subordinates met at Carthage on November 3 and confirmed plans tentatively agreed to several days earlier. If the Fifth Army could advance quickly a dozen miles to the Cassino line, if the army could then break through the Cassino defenses rapidly, and if the army could move ahead 25 miles to the Frosinone area, Eisenhower would authorize an amphibious assault somewhere in the Rome vicinity. Frosinone, about 40 miles below Rome, was reasonably close enough to the capital to make possible a relatively rapid link-up with a beach-head established somewhere near Rome.

In the hope that these conditions could be met, Eisenhower requested the CCS for permission to retain in the theater until December 15 a total of 56 British and 12 American LSTs (landing ships, tank) scheduled for immediate return to England. Only thus, he explained, could he speed the advance in Italy and secure Rome.

The CCS approved the request.

With an amphibious operation at last within the realm of possibility, Eisenhower requested the CCS for a further extension to hold his shipping until January 15. At the same time, on November 8, two months after the Salerno invasion, Eisenhower, for the first time, specifically ordered Alexander to capture Rome. He was calling for an amphibious landing.

Issuing his orders on the same day, Alexander specified the place. It was to be Anzio. The beaches at Anzio, 35 miles below Rome, were suitable for assault landings. The open terrain of the low, level coastal plain around Anzio was favorable for maneuver. From Anzio good roads led to the Alban Hills, about 20 miles inland. Fifteen miles southeast of Rome, rising between the two major highways leading to the capital, and dominating the southern approaches to the city, the Alban Hills comprised the last natural barrier the Germans could use to bar an Allied entry into Rome.

What Alexander ordered the Fifth Army to do was to crack the Cassino line and attack up the valley of the Liri valley to Frosinone, the classical route for an army marching on Rome from the south. When the Fifth Army reached Frosinone, General Clark was to launch a seaborne landing in the Anzio area and move toward the Alban Hills. The advance from Cassino to Frosinone, followed by the thrust toward the Alban Hills from Anzio, Alexander believed, would get the Allies quickly into Rome.

Now it would be up to Mark Clark to make the idea work.

At forty-eight, younger than most officers of his rank, Clark had enjoyed a meteoric rise in the Army. A West Point graduate and wounded in World War I, Clark was a colonel early in 1942 and the Operations Officer of Lieutenant General Lesley J. McNair's Army Ground Forces staff, the headquarters charged with training in the States. In May of that year he became McNair's chief of staff. In June he took command of the American ground forces in the European theater. In November, as Eisenhower's second in command, he made a hazardous submarine voyage to Africa to establish contact with the Free French before the North African landings. He did much to secure French co-operation afterwards.

Aggressive, hard-working, and impatient, Clark was ambitious and frankly so, for he looked on ambition as the goad that spurred a man to considerable exertion and eventual success. He had drive, he was efficient, he enjoyed attracting favorable attention, and he felt impelled constantly to prove his worth. He endeavored to hide his sensibilities behind a mask of coldness. Yet, like most commanders of high rank, he had charm. "Clark impresses me, as always," a senior commander wrote in his diary. "You cannot help but like him."

When the question of creating the Fifth U. S. Army was being discussed in North Africa early in 1943, Eisenhower noted that Clark "was very anxious to have that command instead of his then title of Deputy Commander in Chief." Eisenhower warned Clark that the Fifth Army would be nothing more than a training headquarters for some time. He told Clark that he was thinking of putting Clark in command of a front-line corps. But the title of Army Commander was too attractive. Clark wanted the post, and Eisenhower appointed him commander of the first American army headquarters activated in the European theater, Patton being nominated a short time later to command the Seventh Army for the invasion of Sicily.

A month after his appointment, Clark began to "plague" —Eisenhower's word—Eisenhower for action. Concerned lest the war in the Mediterranean be won before he could lead troops in combat, Clark was, according to Eisenhower, "most unhappy." Clark's chance finally came at Salerno.

Eisenhower had already characterized Clark as "the best organizer, planner and trainer of troops that I have met." It was not long before Eisenhower could call him the "ablest and most experienced officer we have in planning amphibious operations."

At Salerno Clark was conscious that his performance would be measured against that of Patton in Sicily. He knew he would also be judged against the cocky commander of the British Eighth Army, Bernard Montgomery, who had won his reputation at Alamein. In comparison with these commanders, as well as with Alexander, Clark was a late-comer, and because of his relative youth and inexperience, he showed great deference to his British colleagues in Italy.

After Salerno, where he proved his ability to win a battle, Clark became increasingly self-assured, he also became less deferential. Though he maintained his cordiality with his British associates—a strict Eisenhower requirement for American commanders—Clark became disenchanted with them.

He had several reasons. In his opinion, Montgomery had been inexcusably slow in coming up from the toe of Italy while the Salerno battle raged. Had Montgomery moved more quickly, he might have aided Clark. Yet because Alexander's headquarters determined public information policies, the British Broadcasting Corporation announced to the world how Montgomery was racing up the peninsula of Italy to rescue Clark. Nothing, Clark felt—and he was justified in his thinking—was further from the truth.

News releases unmistakably favoring the British were not just, and Clark, who had always had a flair for public relations, determined to counterbalance what he considered to be the prevailing policy. Determined to get justice for his Fifth Army, he surrounded himself, as the campaign progressed, with an ever larger entourage of cameramen and newspaper correspondents who made sure that the accomplishments of his army were recorded and publicized. The crowning achievement and one that he desired ever more ardently to give his army—and incidentally himself—was the glory of liberating Rome.

What particularly bothered Clark was the possibility that Montgomery and his British Eighth Army might win this honor. Though the going was no easier for Montgomery on the east coast, a lateral road across the peninsula from Pescara on that coast led through Avezzano to the back door of Rome. If Montgomery managed to get to Pescara, he could swing down the road to Avezzano and perhaps beat Clark to the capital.

To Clark, this would not be fair. While the British Eighth Army had come into Italy easily, Clark's army had had to battle ashore at Salerno and had thereby earned the right to take Rome.

Though Clark's army contained a British corps as well as

an American corps, the headquarters was indisputably American. And somehow it rankled him that the British elements of his command had reached Naples first. It had been planned that way. But if the British Eighth Army reached Rome first, the Americans, it seemed to Clark, would have been shut out of achievement—the Americans, his Fifth Army, and himself.

The result was an impatience—a brooding, restless impatience—to break the stalemate that threatened to bog down the Fifth Army and deny victory and the crowning glory, the capture of Rome.

Though Clark had been studying the possibility of amphibious operations to speed his progress, Alexander's directive of November 8, which ordered an amphibious descent on Anzio, was disquieting because it solved none of the problems. Yet as Clark thought about the situation, about where the Italian campaign and he were going, he soon became a fervent champion of the Anzio idea. As a matter of fact, in thinking about the future, he came close to a strategic concept talked about by some British planners. The cross-Channel invasion, he began to believe, might perhaps fail. In the event of a disaster like the raid on Dieppe in 1942, OVERLORD would be worse because it was to be bigger. If this occurred, the entire war in Europe might turn into a stalemate. Would it not be better to maintain the threat of a cross-Channel operation while strengthening the forces in Italy for eventual movement into the Balkans? It seemed to make sense. Since the first step toward this course of action was to get to Rome, and since an amphibious operation was the best way to take Rome, Clark threw himself into the Anzio effort with all his might.

Clark's staff came up with a plan for Anzio and christened it SHINGLE. Following Alexander's instructions, the plan called for a landing at Anzio after the Fifth Army reached the vicinity of Frosinone and was ready to launch a full-scale drive toward the Alban Hills. The force at Anzio was to be small. It was to help the major Fifth Army forces capture the Alban hill mass. Juncture of both forces, Clark assumed, would take place no later than seven days after the landing.

Though based on Alexander's directive, Clark's plan made a fundamental change. In Alexander's concept the Anzio force was to take the Alban Hills. In Clark's the roles of the participants were reversed. According to Clark's idea, the main Fifth Army forces driving overland from Frosinone were to capture the Alban Hills.

Reconciling the two concepts had little importance in late November and early December, for the Anzio landing appeared doomed to indefinite postponement. Enemy resistance, mountainous terrain, and bad weather so slowed the Fifth Army that no immediate prospect existed of getting to Frosinone and within supporting distance of the projected landing site. As a matter of fact, the Fifth Army had not yet reached the Cassino line, 25 miles short of Frosinone.

As his troops fought through the mountains in southern Italy, across heights named Camino, Difensa, and Maggiore, as battles raged at San Pietro and on the approaches to San Vittore, as the Fifth Army inched its way across snow-covered peaks, frozen precipices, and slippery gorges, Clark despaired of reaching an adequate supporting distance from which to launch the Anzio landing. Yet, on December 10, he suggested that the amphibious assault be executed nevertheless.

His reasoning was this: the theater had received permission to retain, but not indefinitely, the landing ships and craft needed for the amphibious venture; perhaps the Anzio force could somehow be strengthened; if this force could gain a beachhead and hold it for more than seven days, its mere presence deep in the German rear might break up the incipient stalemate. In other words, by posing a threat to German lines of communication between the main front and Rome, the Anzio force might so dishearten and demoralize the Germans that they would weaken their front, withdraw to face the threat in their rear, and thereby facilitate the Fifth Army's advance to Rome.

The idea was attractive but impractical. Still trying to get to the Cassino line in December, the Fifth Army was much too far from Anzio for a landing to succeed. Nor could troops be spared from the battle flaming on the approaches to that line for an amphibious operation. Beyond the Mignano gap, Mounts Sammucro and Trocchio denied Clark access to ground that appeared suitable for more rapid advance, the Rapido River plain and the Liri River valley. Fighting to the edge of the high ground overlooking the flooded Rapido plain brought the Fifth Army close to exhaustion. By the time the army got to the Cassino line and recovered sufficiently to crack the line, drive to Frosinone, and execute the Anzio invasion—by that time, the ships that Eisenhower had been able to hold for several weeks would have to be released for the other commitments elsewhere. On December 18, Clark reluctantly recommended canceling Anzio.

The amphibious landing at Anzio seemed out of the question. So did prospects for a quick capture of Rome.

THE DECISION

3 TOWARD THE END of November, 1943, when American and British leaders met at Cairo to discuss, among other matters, how to execute OVERLORD while at the same time continuing operations in the Mediterranean, Winston Churchill was discouraged and depressed. The Mediterranean campaign was not going so well as he had hoped. The Allies, he believed, had not assisted the Yugoslav partisans as much as he thought possible. Nor had they extended operations into the eastern Mediterranean with a view to bringing Turkey into the war.

As for Italy, he could not understand why the CCS could not give Eisenhower additional resources to make possible the early capture of Rome and advance to the Pisa–Rimini line. Why not defer for a few weeks longer the scheduled transfer out of the Mediterranean of the landing ships needed for OVERLORD? Why not facilitate an amphibious assault designed to capture Rome?

The answers he wished were not forthcoming, and when the Americans and British traveled to Teheran at the end of the month to meet the Russians, things went from bad to worse— at least for Mr. Churchill. He made eloquent pleas for strengthening the forces in Italy and for extending operations into the Aegean and eastern Mediterranean even at the expense of delaying the cross-Channel attack.

To no avail. Stalin preferred a campaign in western Europe with OVERLORD as the main effort and an invasion of southern France as a subsidiary and complementary operation. If Allied resources were not sufficient to execute both and, in addition, maintain the offensive in Italy, Stalin was willing to see the troops in Italy go over on the defensive.

Churchill objected. Failure to take Rome, he said, would be a crushing defeat. Enough shipping, he argued, ought to be retained in the Mediterranean to enable at least two divisions to make amphibious turning movements to speed a drive on Rome. And though he was willing to accept an invasion of southern France to assist the cross-Channel operation, he wanted some kind of action in the eastern Mediterranean to prod Turkey into entering the war on the Allied side. Turkey, Churchill considered, was the prize.

Greater activity in the Mediterranean depended on one of two alternatives: postpone OVERLORD or withdraw landing craft from the Indian Ocean. Neither course was attractive to the Americans. What seemed advisable to them was concentrating the limited Mediterranean resources in Italy because an invasion of southern France was predicated on the prior fact of reaching a line somewhere north of Rome.

In the ensuing discussion, Churchill again lost out. Stalin supported the Americans and a power thrust across the Channel in the spring of 1944, together with a simultaneous invasion of southern France launched from Mediterranean resources. Yet, to satisfy Churchill, the CCS permitted Eisenhower to retain until January 15, 1944, a total of 68 LSTs scheduled for transfer to England. This permission was, in reality, a meaningless gesture. An amphibious assault along the Italian coast could not possibly be launched in the few weeks remaining before that date.

During the concluding Anglo-American discussions in Cairo in early December, the Allied leaders confirmed the Teheran decisions—the cross-Channel and southern France invasions were to be the "supreme operations for 1944." Nothing was to be done anywhere in the world to jeopardize their success.

The definite decision for OVERLORD brought major command changes in the Mediterranean. Most important was the appointment of Eisenhower as Supreme Commander, Allied Expeditionary Force for the invasion of northwest Europe. Though the CCS were willing to permit Eisenhower to remain in the Mediterranean until the capture of Rome, Eisenhower himself saw no immediate prospect of taking the capital. The static battle, the winter weather, the solid German defensive line, and the dearth of landing craft for outflanking movements killed immediate hope, he thought, of gaining Rome.

As a further corollary of the definite decision for OVERLORD, the British command in the Middle East was merged with the Allied command in the Mediterranean, and General Sir H. Maitland Wilson, the British Middle East commander became the Supreme Allied Commander of the expanded theater. He was, in effect, Eisenhower's replacement. Lieutenant General Jacob Devers, transferred from England, became Wilson's deputy and commander of the U. S. troops. Tedder was selected for transfer to England as Eisenhower's deputy, while Montgomery was to leave his Eighth Army in Italy in order to take command of an army group in England for the cross-Channel invasion. All the changes were to go into effect at the end of 1943.

One of the consequences of the command changes was to give the British executive direction of the Mediterranean theater, making the theater, in effect, a British province. While Eisenhower had commanded the Mediterranean forces, Roosevelt and Marshall had had the controlling voice in decisions affecting the theater. With Wilson in command, Churchill and Brooke would have the final say. Churchill would obviously be able to play a more direct role in the conduct of the Italian campaign. When Marshall passed executive control to

Brooke, the Prime Minister virtually took command of the operations in the Mediterranean.

According to American practice, the theater commander was a rather independent figure. He operated under the supervision of his superiors—in Eisenhower's case the CCS—but the function of the higher headquarters was guidance rather than command. In British practice, the supervision exercised by the higher echelon was quite close. In essence, a British theater commander was the creature of the British Chiefs of Staff. Somewhat like Clemenceau, who believed warfare too important to be entrusted to generals, the British chiefs felt that operations were too vital to be entirely confided to the judgment of the field commanders. And the British chiefs were, of course, immediately subordinate to Mr. Churchill.

The command changes in the Mediterranean had their effect on General Alexander. Too finely schooled, too superbly self-controlled to show disappointment, irritation, or resentment, Alexander nevertheless had hoped either to replace Eisenhower as Supreme Allied Commander in the Mediterranean or to move to England to become part of the main action in Europe. Italy, his area, was increasingly becoming a sideshow that, because of the relatively small resources allocated to it, could have no decisive effect on the outcome of the war.

Clark, for his part, was not immediately affected by the alterations in command. President Roosevelt encouraged him to get to Rome, and General Marshall told him he would like to have Rome before the cross-Channel attack was launched —for its blow against German morale. After Rome, Clark learned, he was to leave his Fifth Army in Italy, take command of the Seventh Army still in Sicily (Patton would be recalled to England), and lead the invasion of southern France.

Flattered, Clark was nevertheless realist enough to know there was little prospect of getting to Rome and bringing the Italian campaign to a close unless German resistance suddenly collapsed. There was no sign of collapse. The alternative method of getting to Rome, an amphibious landing in the Rome area, was simply not feasible because the Fifth Army could not get to and through the Cassino line and up the Liri valley to within reasonable supporting distance and because shortages of shipping prevented an amphibious operation in the strength deemed necessary. In this situation, Clark figured he would stay in Italy until about February 1, then leave to take charge of the preparations to invade southern France, meanwhile making every effort to take Rome.

At this point, one of those completely accidental but none-theless momentous occurrences in the affairs of men took place. Mr. Churchill became ill. As a direct result of that happening, the whole Italian campaign underwent a profound change.

The Allied conferences at Cairo and Teheran had tired Mr. Churchill mentally and physically. The defeat of his poli-cies had temporarily dispirited him. Departing from Egypt on December 11 by air, he planned to spend a night at Eisen-hower's headquarters in Tunis, then visit Alexander and Mont-gomery in Italy. But when he arrived in Tunis, he felt, in his own words, at the end of his tether. Physically exhausted, worn out, drained of energy, he went to bed. The doctors pro-nounced it pneumonia.

For more than a week Churchill was seriously sick. When he began to recover, though he had to remain in bed, he was able to work after a fashion. He read messages and papers and dispatched telegrams and instructions.

While lying in bed, Churchill had ample time to review the events that had led to the abortion of his strategy. The balance had swung definitely away from the Mediterranean toward the American cross-Channel concept.

Was his defeat irrevocable? Or could he do something to gain some sort of victory?

He did nothing until Brooke arrived in Tunis on December 19. Only a day earlier, Clark had recommended shelving Anzio.

Returning from Montgomery's headquarters in Italy, Brooke spent a few hours with his chief, still weak, still abed, but with an idea.

Churchill discussed with Brooke what might be salvaged from the wreckage of British strategic aspirations. "We agreed on the policy," Churchill later wrote, "and also that while I should deal with the commanders on the spot, he would do his best to overcome all difficulties at home."

What was the policy?

Soon after Brooke left by air for London, Churchill sent a telegram to his Chiefs of Staff. He made two points: "the stagnation of the whole campaign on the Italian Front is becoming scandalous"; and landing craft had not been put to the slightest combat use for at least three months, also a scandalous condition.

Three days later, on December 22, his Chiefs of Staff replied. They agreed that amphibious equipment in the Mediterranean should be used to open the way for a rapid advance on Rome. The trouble was the number of vessels in the theater —they could transport only one division, whereas two were needed.

"Resigned to Turkish neutrality" by his own admission on December 23, a failure he took very hard, forced into admitting the necessity for an invasion of southern France, a course of action he agreed to with great reluctance, and compelled to accept the impossibility of operations in the eastern Mediterranean, a great disappointment, Churchill became bound and determined to have Rome—"we must have the big Rome amphibious operation. . . . In no case can we sacrifice Rome for the Riviera."

One of the real difficulties was the fact that while the British continued to think of provoking decisive action in Italy, Eisenhower was no longer interested. He was looking forward to OVERLORD. If there was one thing he wished in the Mediterranean, it was the invasion of southern France because of its expected assistance to the cross-Channel effort. And perhaps that could be launched even though the Allies were still south of Rome.

The commander who stood to gain from the capture of Rome was Alexander. Rome might well make up for his failure to get a new command and a promotion. Alexander told Churchill he wanted Rome, but only after Churchill prodded him. Alexander also said he wanted Anzio. But he wanted a two-division lift as well. And how could he get that?

Bedell Smith, who was to accompany Eisenhower to England, agreed that Anzio was the best means of getting to Rome. But he, too, had no idea of where to get the additional landing craft. Even if they turned up, how could they be held in the theater without jeopardizing the success of OVER-LORD?

Why not keep the LSTs until February 15? Churchill asked.

According to Churchill, Smith said he could not bear to ask the CCS for a third extension.

Churchill had no such compunction. Anzio held out too much promise—to bring glory to what had rapidly become a sideshow; to allay Alexander's disappointment by giving him the opportunity to gain a spectacular victory; and to raise the morale of the troops in Italy by giving them a meaningful objective.

Rome became a last gasp of British strategy, for its capture would make possible a quick movement to northern Italy, possibly a turn eastward into the Balkans or westward into southern France, perhaps even make OVERLORD unnecessary.

It was a dazzling vision.

On Christmas Eve, Churchill talked late into the night about Anzio with Wilson, Alexander, Tedder, and some of

their staff officers—all British. All agreed on the necessity for
an Anzio landing in at least two-division strength with a target
date around January 20. This meant that the theater needed to
hold back for three weeks, until February 5, at least 56 LSTs
scheduled to be released earlier. "On this," Churchill telegraphed the British Chiefs of Staff, "depends the success or
ruin of our Italian campaign."

On Christmas morning the same British officers met with
Churchill, along with Admiral Sir John Cunningham who,
having replaced his cousin, now commanded the Allied naval
forces in the Mediterranean. This time several Americans were
also present, including Eisenhower and Bedell Smith. All agreed
on the desirability of an Anzio landing and on the need to
have nothing less than an initial assault of two divisions.

A telegram on December 25 apprised President Roosevelt of the meeting, of the agreement, and of the necessity to
have Roosevelt's approval to retain the required LSTs until
February 5. Otherwise, Churchill assured the President, "the
Italian battle [will] stagnate and fester on for another three
months." He admitted his liberty in assuming that Roosevelt
would agree. For he had already issued orders to Alexander to
prepare for the operation "accordingly." He explained to
Roosevelt what was at stake: "If this opportunity is not grasped
we must expect the ruin of the Mediterranean campaign of
1944."

Two days later Churchill flew from Tunis to Marrakesh,
Morocco, for three weeks' convalescence, "bearing," as he
said, "my burdens with me."

His burdens were many. Among them was an uneasy
sense of discomfort, perhaps of guilt, because of what he had
just put over. Despite the promise made at Cairo-Teheran that
nothing would be permitted to interfere with OVERLORD
and southern France, he had pushed through a course of action
inconsistent with his earlier commitment.

He had fired up Alexander. He had dragged along Eisenhower and Smith, who had been most reluctant, in view of

their impending departure, to influence the discussions and who had consequently refrained from active participation in the decision. He had convinced Wilson—but Wilson had no intimate knowledge of the Italian campaign, was unfamiliar with the problems of the Mediterranean theater, and had taken the part virtually of an observer, saying "merely that it sounded like a good idea to go around them rather than be bogged down in the mountains."

Churchill had had the great advantage of being ill. How could his subordinates resist him when he needed to be humored and cheered? How could they oppose a course of action on which their chief had already made up his mind?

Churchill had also brushed aside the objections of Eisenhower's intelligence officer, Brigadier K. W. D. Strong. A British officer, Strong did not favor the Anzio operation. He judged the German forces in Italy too numerous. But Churchill had not permitted him to state his opposition until after the decision had been made. "Well," Mr. Churchill had then said, "we may as well hear the seamy side of the question." Discussion of the intelligence factor was short.

Finally, Brooke had been absent, Brooke who could anchor Churchill's enthusiasms on the rock of practicality.

Yet Churchill believed sincerely in the Mediterranean area for active campaigning. And if Mr. Roosevelt supported him—how could an old friend like Roosevelt not support him? —he would be able to give the troops in the Mediterranean a sense of purpose and the opportunity to attain the single objective that remained valid and possible in the entire area. Even if the capture of Rome did not open the way to the delightful vistas lying east and west of northern Italy, it would give the Germans a damaging body blow that would soften them for the cross-Channel smash to the chin.

Churchill had not consulted Clark. But he probably knew that no proselyting was needed to convert Clark to the cause of Anzio.

As a matter of fact, Clark was of two minds. The many

imponderables impressed him—the shipping, the weakened main front remaining after the Anzio force was withdrawn from the line, the distance that would separate the Anzio force from the main front, the German strength. Could the Allies afford another Salerno? The possibility of getting to Rome was tempting, but the risk looked tremendous.

Yet the opportunity was, in the end, too attractive, and Clark's ambition got the better of him. When he received word immediately after Christmas of the decision in favor of Anzio, Clark was delighted. He asked to be relieved of responsibility for planning the invasion of southern France so he could remain in Italy at the head of his Fifth Army. His troops by then were within sight of the Cassino line. Perhaps the Anzio landing would work. But his request to be absolved of responsibility for southern France was disapproved.

Meanwhile, Clark worked closely with his planners and with Alexander. He encouraged his superior and badgered his subordinates to try to make the operation feasible.

In Marrakesh, the day after Churchill's arrival, on December 28, he received the telegram he eagerly awaited from Roosevelt. The President did not disappoint him. He agreed to delaying the departure of the 56 LSTs scheduled for OVERLORD. The Anzio operation, then, was on.

On the same day, Churchill received Alexander's plan for the landing. Alexander had conferred with Clark, he informed Churchill, and both had agreed that one American division and one British division should make up the initial assault force, plus paratroopers and Commandos. All the troops would operate under an American corps headquarters. The assault would be launched January 22. Ten days before the landing, Clark would open a full-scale attack to pin down the Germans on the main front and divert them from the Anzio area.

Yet all was not settled. Despite Roosevelt's acquiescence, rumblings began to be heard from the technicians—the operational planners, the logisticians. According to news that reached Clark on New Year's Day, several of Eisenhower's principal staff officers felt that Alexander was "badly off base" in promoting the amphibious maneuver. Unless Alexander and Clark could show that Anzio would not interfere with the projected invasion of southern France, Anzio would undoubtedly be canceled.

"Genuinely eager" for Anzio, as he admitted, Clark tried to help the idea along on January 2 by sending a message to Alexander. Perhaps, Clark thought, Alexander could use the written expression, if he wished, as another piece of evidence in favor of the amphibious operation.

The Anzio landing, Clark wrote, would surely "exercise a decisive influence on the operation to capture Rome." It would, he repeated, outflank the Cassino line anchored on the Garigliano and Rapido Rivers. Whether the 70 miles between Anzio and Cassino was too great a distance for action on one front to influence the other was a risk they could not avoid. Though an amphibious landing closer to the main front would permit greater co-ordination of the two attacks, it would be too close for any strategic gain. A direct threat against Rome had to be mounted, and in Clark's opinion Anzio would do the job.

Though the issue was yet to be finally decided, Alexander and Clark continued their planning. On January 3 they asked Churchill whether they might retain the single American parachute regiment remaining in the theater. The regiment was supposed to go to England for OVERLORD, but they wished to use it at Anzio.

Churchill obliged them. Appealing for and securing the necessary concurrence, Churchill overcame another hurdle.

Still another obstacle reared up on January 4. According to a telegram from Alexander, he and Clark needed Churchill's "help and assistance" once more. The problem was this: Clark required a few more LSTs, fourteen to be exact, in order to nourish the Anzio force until it joined hands with the main

Fifth Army forces. And an additional ten LSTs for only fifteen days beyond February 5 in order to strengthen the two assault divisions with artillery, tanks, and other supporting arms. Though Alexander and Clark were "willing," as Alexander said, "to accept any risks to achieve our object," they needed these additional vessels. Though they realized that this request interfered "to some extent" with preparations for invading southern France, "surely the prize is worth it."

Churchill agreed. The prize was worth it. He secured what was asked for.

During these days early in 1944 military experts in London and Washington were busy making calculations of the global resources with a view to possible reallocations among the various theaters. One of the results of the rearrangements accomplished was the discovery that certain shifts of units and equipment beneficial to Italy could be made. In the spring, additional American divisions from the United States, more French divisions from North Africa, and further British-controlled divisions from the Middle East would become available for employment in Italy. At the same time, sufficient men and equipment would be on hand in England to make possible the cross-Channel attack.

In North Africa—at Marrakesh—a final act on Anzio took place in two scenes. The first was a conference on January 7 with Wilson, Cunningham, Alexander, Devers, Bedell Smith, and others in attendance on Churchill. Devers, just arrived in the theater from England to take up his duties as Wilson's deputy, found the meeting "a unique experience." He did not understand why the conference was necessary—surely a simple military decision, it seemed to him, could be reached without recourse to eloquent discussion. But he had no fault to find with the results of the talking. He believed, as he said, "the answers that came out of it were correct."

The second scene occurred the next day, January 8, when another conference was held. At this one there was no need for Churchill to be actively engaged. Alexander and Cunningham did most of the talking.

At the conclusion, a beaming Churchill, virtually recovered from his pneumonia and malaise, triumphantly wired President Roosevelt that "unanimous agreement for action as proposed was reached by the responsible officers of both countries and of all services."

Having completely recovered his physical well-being and his normal high spirits, Churchill departed from Africa on January 14. He had won a victory. Anzio was on the books.

Now it was up to those who had become convinced in one fashion or another and for a variety of reasons to prove that it could in actuality be done. All the problems had not been solved. The risks were enormous. But maybe just this kind of gamble would pay off.

The exact German reaction to a landing at Anzio was, of course, impossible to predict. But the most probable responses were all desirable from the Allied point of view. By cutting the German main line of communications south of Rome, the Anzio force might prompt the Germans at the Cassino line to withdraw. Even the mere presence of a large Allied force in the German rear and the threat these troops would pose to the German communications might be enough to compel German withdrawal. Or the Germans might find it necessary to weaken the Cassino front in order to meet the Anzio threat, and in so doing open the way for an Allied drive up the Liri valley toward Rome.

Thus, the Anzio force had to be strong enough not only to cut or genuinely threaten German communications but to sustain itself independently until the main forces followed up the expected German wihtdrawal and made contact with the beachhead. Yet the slim Mediterranean resources in men and ships continued to limit the size of the operation, while OVERLORD hung like Damocles' sword over the planning—the projected release of landing ships and craft, plus other naval vessels, required the assault to come off quickly or not at all.

Working at top speed, the planners and responsible commanders nevertheless assembled a sizable force. Under the VI Corps headquarters, two divisions, three Ranger battalions, two Commando battalions, a parachute regiment, and an additional parachute battalion were to assault the Anzio beaches on January 22, 1944.

According to Alexander's instructions, the Anzio force was to make its landing "with the object of cutting the enemy lines of communication and threatening the rear of the Germans [defending the Cassino line along the Garigliano and Rapido Rivers]." To support the amphibious assault, Clark was to make a strong thrust on the main front through Cassino toward Frosinone "shortly prior to the assault landing to draw in enemy reserves which might be employed against the landing forces and then to create a breach in his front through which every opportunity will be taken to link up rapidly with the seaborne operation."

Unlike Eisenhower's intelligence officers, Alexander's staff members were quite optimistic. They judged that the Germans had about two divisions in reserve near Rome, which was correct. And they counted on the weather and the Allied air forces to interfere with the movement of German reinforcements to the beachhead. It seemed hardly likely that the Germans could successfully oppose the landing.

Ten days before the operation was to begin, Alexander reminded Clark of the object of the landing. The Anzio force, Alexander repeated, was "to cut the enemy's main communications in the Colli Laziali [another name for the Alban Hills] area Southeast of Rome, and to threaten the [German] rear."

As Alexander saw the prospective results, the landing would compel the Germans to react to the threat by weakening their Cassino defenses. Clark was then to take advantage of this by striking immediately through those defenses. In other words, Alexander expected the Anzio landing so to frighten the Germans that they would have to pull back from Cassino. Anzio was to pry loose the defensive line along the Garigliano and Rapido Rivers.

As Clark interpreted Alexander's directive, the Fifth Army was "(a) To seize and secure a beachhead in the vicinity of Anzio. (b) Advance on Colli Laziali [the Alban Hills]." What seemed on the surface to be perfectly clear—a mission to be executed in two logically consecutive parts—was in reality deliberately vague on the second part. The VI Corps was to establish a beachhead—no question about that—but was it then to advance *toward* the Alban Hills or *to* them?

The reason for the deliberate vagueness was Clark's desire to keep the VI Corps flexible. Clark did not want to commit the corps to a single unalterable line of action. For he could not prejudge the German reaction at Anzio. And he was not sure he could get through the Cassino line and up the Liri valley to join with the Anzio force as quickly as Alexander seemed to think he could.

Clark's intelligence officers were less optimistic than Alexander's. They believed that the seriousness of the threat posed by the landing would force the Germans to react violently. For a landing at Anzio, they felt, would be "an emergency to be met by all the resources and strength available to the German High Command in Italy." As soon as the Germans appreciated the magnitude of the Anzio landing, as soon as they realized that the Allies could not launch other attacks at other points along the coast, they would—Clark's intelligence officers believed—make a ruthless concentration of forces against the beachhead. For the Germans could not let the Anzio force move to the Alban Hills and threaten the safety of the entire Tenth Army. Otherwise, a withdrawal from southern Italy would become necessary, bringing to an end the successful defense that had been so impressive.

Fifth Army intelligence officers judged the Germans to

have immediately near Rome to counter the Anzio landing a corps headquarters and two divisions, plus contingents of paratroopers and tanks. By the third day of the invasion, the Germans could probably commit an additional division drawn from the Adriatic front facing the British Eighth Army. Within the next two weeks, the Germans, in all likelihood, would have secured from other areas, from northern Italy perhaps, two more divisions.

As a result of this estimate of German strength, Clark's planners assumed that the VI Corps would meet strong resistance at the beaches and heavy counterattacks as soon as the Germans became aware of the extent and the purport of the operation. Looking back on the Salerno landings, they expected the same pattern of opposition to develop at Anzio. To avoid the perils of Salerno, they turned the emphasis to defense—the troops at Anzio were to dig in as soon as they secured a beachhead; the VI Corps was to maintain a strong force in reserve to meet the German attacks.

To help the VI Corps hold its ground, Clark augmented the Anzio troop list. Additional vessels were becoming available by virtue of Mr. Churchill's persuasion and largesse, and it became possible to strengthen the landing force. The initial Anzio force had consisted of the 3rd U. S. Division, the 1st British Division, the 504th U. S. Parachute Infantry Regiment, the 509th U. S. Parachute Infantry Battalion, a British Special Service Brigade of two Commando battalions, and the U. S. Ranger Force of three battalions. A week before the operation Clark made available also the major part of the 1st U. S. Armored Division, a regiment of the 45th U. S. Division, and more artillery. If even greater strength proved to be necessary, Clark was prepared to send the remainder of the 1st Armored and 45th Infantry Divisions to the beachhead.

The initial force earmarked for Anzio had thus grown from a tentative figure of 24,000 men under the original conception to an expected eventual strength of more than 110,000.

From a subsidiary operation on the left flank of a nearby Fifth Army, the Anzio landing had developed into a major operation deep in the German rear. As part of the broadened concept, the British Eighth Army was to make a strong feint on its front along the east coast of Italy, while the Fifth Army was to launch a strong attack against the Cassino line.

In addition to pinning down the Germans and preventing them from immediately reinforcing the defenders at Anzio, Clark hoped to break through the Garigliano-Rapido defenses. If he could precipitate a German withdrawal from Cassino, the Anzio invasion might turn the retirement into a rout.

To these ends Clark planned a three-corps attack against the Cassino line. The French Expeditionary Corps on the right was to lead off on January 12. The U. S. II Corps was to add its weight three days later. The British X Corps was then to strike across the lower Garigliano, making one thrust on the 17th, another on the 19th. On the 20th, the U. S. II Corps was to assault across the Rapido in the shadow of the height of Monte Cassino, still held by the Germans. Two days later the climax would come with the VI Corps landing at Anzio.

Clark expected the VI Corps, once ashore, to go over immediately to the defensive. But in the unlikely event that the opposition was slight, the corps was to advance "on" the Alban Hills by one of two routes, either directly up the Albano road to cut Highway 7 leading to Rome, or by way of Cisterna to cut not only Highway 7 but also Highway 6 at the head of the Liri valley, at Valmontone. Whether the VI Corps defended or attacked after landing would depend on how the corps commander sized up the situation and on how he personally decided to act.

The corps commander was Major General John P. Lucas, destined to be one of the unfortunate and tragic figures of World War II.

THE LANDING

4   GENERAL LUCAS was an old man at fifty-four. In mid-January, 1944, noting his birthday, he wrote in his diary, "I am afraid I feel every year of it."

He was also tired. Directing the VI Corps during four months of arduous mountain warfare in Italy had worn him out.

His colleagues did not notice his fatigue. A friend who had not seen Lucas for some time remarked that he was the "same Lucas." He looked "like an old man, but then he has looked that way for a good many years."

Slow of movement, appearing smaller than he was in actuality, Lucas had a slight greyish mustache and smoked a corncob pipe.

As commander of the 3rd Division in the United States, Lucas had attracted General Marshall's attention and respect. Sent to the Mediterranean early in 1943 as an observer, Lucas acted as Marshall's eyes and ears for several weeks. When he reported back to Marshall, he received command of a corps in the States. But he was soon reassigned to North Africa again, this time to help Eisenhower, for Marshall thought it would be good for a young commander like Eisenhower to have an older and more mature officer like Lucas close by.

Lucas had "military stature, prestige, and experience," according to Marshall. Easy-going, likeable, and patient, Lucas was also shrewd and observant. During the campaign in Sicily, as Eisenhower's "American Deputy," an unofficial title, he commuted between Patton's Seventh Army headquarters on the island and Eisenhower's headquarters in Algiers, acting, according to his own statement, as Eisenhower's "personal representative with the combat troops."

At the end of the campaign in Sicily, when Lieutenant General Omar N. Bradley was transferred to England to take command of the First Army in preparation for the OVERLORD invasion, Lucas took his place as commander of the II Corps. A month later, after the stiff battle of Salerno had cost the VI Corps commander his job, Lucas was brought over from Sicily to take command of that corps. Since then he had directed the VI Corps in the Italian campaign with great competence.

Cautious and thorough by temperament, Lucas was well qualified to conduct mountain warfare. He was flattered when Clark told him, "You know how to fight in the mountains." Maybe he did, he admitted, but he had already had a bellyful.

The truth was that Lucas wished to be daring and imaginative. He admired the grand maneuver, the bold gesture. But he was aware of his own limitations. When the conversation at dinner one evening turned on what Napoleon might have done to hasten the Italian campaign, Lucas admitted he wished he knew. "I am just a poor working girl," he said, "trying to get ahead." The only thing he was sure of—"Wars should be fought in better country than this."

Shortly before the Salerno invasion, when Lucas took note of the risks involved, he marveled at Clark's composure. Clark, Lucas wrote in his diary, "is certainly not afraid to take rather desperate chances," then added, "which, after all, is the only way to win a war." Lucas went on to say, "He is probably risking his official neck but it doesn't seem to bother him much."

In almost daily entries in his diary, Lucas set down his problems—"everything has gone to hell"; his apprehensions—"Am running this thing on a shoestring, and a thin little shoestring at that"; and his great love for the American soldier:

I must keep from thinking of the fact that my order will send these men into a desperate attack.

I think too often of my men out in the mountains. I am far too tenderhearted ever to be a success at my chosen profession.

I don't see how our men stand what they do . . . they are the finest soldiers in the world and none but an humble man should command them. My constant prayer to Almighty God is that I may have the wisdom to bring them through this ordeal with the maximum of success and the minimum loss of life.

His relations with Clark, he noted, were amiable and pleasant. "As long as I win battles," he added, "I imagine they will be."

Unpretentious, he could write: "I am blessed in all my subordinates. They do all the work and most of the thinking."

Lucas learned about the plan for the Anzio landing late in December, when Clark told him he intended to pull the VI Corps out of the line in the near future to enable the staff and assigned units to prepare for the amphibious landing. Lucas had an immediate reaction. He urged Clark to speed up plans to relieve the corps headquarters so he, Lucas, would be sure to have enough time to get ready. The corps pulled back on January 3, as French troops took responsibility for that portion of the line.

Lucas had mixed feelings about Anzio. Though flattered by the opportunity presented to him, he was concerned about the risks involved, an inordinate number to his mind. He was a soldier and would therefore do his duty. But he had a singular lack of enthusiasm for the idea. He needed, he felt, more ships and men, more time to plan, prepare, and rehearse.

Like everybody else concerned with Anzio, Lucas grappled first with the problem of getting enough landing craft and ships. "Unless we can get what we want," he wrote in his diary, "the operation becomes such a desperate undertaking that it should not, in my opinion, be attempted."

If he could not get sufficient shipping to transport him and his troops, "a crack on the chin is certain."

He would, of course, comply with orders, "but these 'Battles of the Little Big Horn' aren't much fun and a failure now would ruin Clark, probably kill me, and certainly prolong the war."

Lucas attended what he called a "high-powered" conference on January 9, the day after the final decision had been reached at Marrakesh. Having been immersed in the day-to-day details of fighting in the mountains, he did not know about Churchill's meetings. Nor did he understand the relationship between Anzio and OVERLORD and the consequent need for haste. Reluctant to go through with the operation, he wished he had been consulted in advance, he knew he could not change the decision, and he felt very strongly his obligation as a soldier to carry out orders.

His impressions of the meeting on January 9, when Alexander presided over a group of commanders and staff officers, revealed his own uncertain state of mind:

Apparently Shingle has become the most important operation in the present scheme of things. Sir Harold started the conference by stating that the operation would take place on January 22 with the troops as scheduled and that there would be no more discussion of these points. He quoted Mr. Churchill as saying, "It will astonish the world," and added, "it will certainly frighten Kesselring." I felt like a lamb being led to the slaughter but thought I was entitled to one bleat so I registered a protest against the target

date as it gave me too little time for rehearsal. This is vital to the
success of anything as terribly complicated as this. I was ruled
down, as I knew I would be, many reasons being advanced as to
the necessity for this speed. The real reasons cannot be military.

I have the bare minimum of ships and craft. The ones that are
sunk [during the operation] cannot be replaced. The force that can
be gotten ashore in a hurry is weak and I haven't sufficient artillery
to hold me over but, on the other hand, I will have more air support than any similar operation ever had before. A week of fine
weather at the proper time and I will make it.

After the conference Alexander drew him aside. "We have
every confidence in you," Alexander told him. "That is why
you were picked."

Lucas was not reassured. To him "the whole affair has a
strong odor of Gallipoli and apparently the same amateur was
still on the coach's bench."

What troubled Lucas most of all was the short time he
had for preparations. Less than two weeks remained between
the conference of January 9 and the operation scheduled for
the 22nd. And he could not seem to get his superiors to understand that the amphibious assault had to be made with well-
trained troops.

His superiors appeared to him to be nonchalant. In actuality, the definite schedule for the cross-Channel attack left
them no choice. Thus, Lucas's urgent demands for more training time were met with what he considered to be indifference.

Assured that both divisions tapped for the initial assault
were experienced in amphibious techniques, Lucas remarked
that the 1st British Division had landed on the island of Pantel-
leria more than six months earlier against no opposition and
had not seen action since then. The 3rd U. S. Division, which
had landed in Sicily in July, had met opposition on the beaches
and had hardly been out of action since that time. The
turnover of infantry lieutenants, Lucas noted—those killed,

wounded, and captured—totaled 115 per cent of authorized strength. "The men that knew the answers," he wrote in his diary, "were gone."

Yet the two divisions selected for the initial assault were good ones, and Lucas knew it. The trouble was time "so pitifully short." There was not enough time for adequate training, and "the Higher Levels just can't see that."

Lucas did not remember what Patton had told him a few days before the invasion of Sicily, more than six months earlier. Patton had said and Lucas had recorded in his diary that a landing operation, in Patton's opinion, required little training. What the troops had to learn was to move straight inland after being put ashore. This method, Patton admitted, resulted in high losses, but an amphibious assault made a great many casualties inevitable anyway.

The final rehearsal of the landing took place on January 19, three days before the real thing, and the results bore out Lucas's pessimism. Coming ashore on the beaches of Pozzuoli Bay near Naples, ground as near like Anzio as could be found, the assault divisions made one mistake after another. The naval forces bringing them to shore bungled. Everything went wrong. The British were bad, the 3rd Division "terrible." As a consequence of mismanagement and ineptitude, about forty DUKWs (amphibious trucks used to bring men and matériel ashore during a landing) and ten artillery pieces, 105-mm. howitzers, were lost in the sea.

Outraged by the confusion and the losses, Clark made known his displeasure in no uncertain terms. Though the naval authorities promised to take corrective measures at once, little could be done in the short time remaining before the operation. The only consolation was hope that a poor dress rehearsal presaged a fine opening night.

Despite the discouraging showing of the invasion force, Cunningham, the naval commander in the Mediterranean, assured Lucas he would have little trouble at Anzio. "The chances are seventy to thirty," Cunningham said, "that, by the time you reach Anzio, the Germans will be north of Rome."

Lucas had a dry comment in his diary. "Apparently everyone was in on the secret of the German intentions except me."

He often wondered whether higher headquarters had intelligence information not available to him. Were there indications that the Germans intended to pull out and move north of Rome? There must be, he told himself in some desperation. Otherwise, why go through with an amphibious assault that had so much inherent promise of failure?

Yet, if the Germans intended to retire from Cassino to positions north of Rome, all the more reason for making a strong end run with well-trained and well-equipped forces able to intercept and destroy the withdrawing troops. But, in Lucas's opinion, he lacked the strength to do so.

When Alexander said that Anzio would make the cross-Channel invasion unnecessary, Lucas was shocked by the exaggeration. He saw no basis for such optimism, and he felt cheated by the fact that he had not been drawn into the apparent knowledge and confidence of his superiors.

Despite his feelings of uncertainty, he was upset when he learned that Clark was planning to establish a small Fifth Army command post near him at Anzio. "I wish to hell he wouldn't," he wrote in his diary. Though Clark was seeking only to give Lucas assurance of his intention to make Anzio a success and to be on hand for the expected juncture of the Anzio troops with those trying to crack through the Cassino line, Lucas interpreted Clark's action as a lack of confidence in the corps commander. "I don't need any help," he wrote with some resentment.

Increasingly, he found himself out of sympathy and out of touch with the thinking going on at the higher echelons. "Army has gone nuts again," he wrote.

The general idea seems to be that the Germans are licked and are fleeing in disorder and nothing remains but to mop up. The only reason for such a belief is that we have recently been able to advance a few miles against them [in the Cassino area] with comparative ease. The Hun has pulled back a bit but I haven't seen the desperate fighting I have during the last four months without learning something. We are not (repeat not) in Rome yet.

Nor was that the worst of it.

They will end up by putting me ashore with inadequate forces and get me in a serious jam. Then, who will take the blame.

On January 20, in an ambivalent frame of mind, General Lucas boarded the U.S.S. *Biscayne* for the voyage to Anzio. "I have many misgivings," he wrote in his diary, "but am also optimistic." The weather was good, and if the weather conditions continued so for four or five days, Lucas wrote, "I should be all right." The Germans did not seem to have discovered the Anzio preparations and the existence of the invasion fleet. "I think we have a good chance to make a killing." Yet he remained apprehensive because he still believed his assault troops lacked sufficient training.

His final thought leaned toward hopelessness:

I wish the higher levels were not so over-optimistic. The Fifth Army is attacking violently toward the Cassino line and has sucked many German troops to the south and the high command seems to think they will stay there. I don't see why. They can slow us up there and move against me at the same time.

General Lucas's worries on the eve of the Anzio landing came not only from his own physical and mental fatigue but also from the inclination of a sensitive man to worry because things were now unalterably fixed. The preparations, for better or worse, were finished. No deficiencies, real or imagined, could be remedied. Nothing further could be done except to execute the assignment. There was no turning back.

On these grounds Lucas might well have dismissed worrisome thoughts. But part of his uncertainty arose from two events that had occurred shortly before his embarkation for Anzio.

The first was a visit from the Fifth Army Operations Officer, Brigadier General Donald W. Brann, on January 12. Brann delivered personally to Lucas the newly issued and final Fifth Army order for the Anzio operation. He had come to see Lucas, Brann explained, in order to discuss the vague wording of the order with respect to Lucas's advance "on" the Alban Hills.

Brann made it clear that Lucas had the primary mission of seizing and securing a beachhead. Clark expected no more. Much thought had gone into phrasing the order because Clark did not want to force Lucas into pushing on to the Alban hill mass at the risk of sacrificing his corps. If conditions warranted moving to the heights, of course, Lucas was free to take advantage of them. But this possibility appeared slim. Clark did not think it possible for Lucas to reach the hill mass and at the same time hold the beachhead to protect the port and the landing beaches. Since loss of the port and the landing beaches would sever completely the link between the Anzio force and the main Fifth Army forces, since Lucas's corps at Anzio would be isolated and at the mercy of the Germans if he lost his supply base, Clark was interested primarily in a beachhead.

The second event flowed from and contributed to this line of reasoning. In an early plan, the 504th Parachute Infantry Regiment was scheduled to make an airborne drop on the Anzio–Albano road about ten miles north of Anzio. This clearly reflected an intention to reach and take the Alban Hills.

Unfortunately, some British commanders objected to the presence of paratroopers behind enemy lines on the ground that they might mistake the Americans for Germans and take them under fire. Naval officers pointed out also that the paratroopers would be within range of naval guns supporting the landing and that the relatively flat terrain of the Anzio coastal plain offered little cover against naval shellfire. Air officers, for their part, could not spare planes for a rehearsal, noted that the troops had not practiced a landing for several months, felt that the whole operation had an air of improvisation, expected the parachutists to be widely dispersed, ineffective, and useless after a drop, and deplored the absence of moonlight, a desirable condition for an airborne attack, at the time of the landing. As the result of these objections, the parachute drop had been canceled. The paratroopers would come into Anzio across the beaches immediately after the infantry assault divisions.

Removing a powerful incentive for pushing the corps out from the landing beaches in order to make contact with the paratroopers thus coincided with doubts expressed by Brann and Clark that Lucas could do more than seize and secure a beachhead. Since Lucas himself had reservations on the strength and the training of the troops under him, he had no doubt that a successful landing and subsequent capture of a beachhead would represent a successful operation.

This was quite different from the earlier conception of an Anzio operation. In November, when the Fifth Army headquarters was making its original plan to comply with Alexander's directive of November 8, both Operations and Intelligence staff officers had agreed on the vital necessity of capturing two places as quickly as possible: the port of Anzio, for its capacity to handle the supplies needed by the forces landed; and the Alban Hills, for its "commanding position" over the Anzio area.

This was in accord with Alexander's concept. Yet Clark in contrast, visualizing the Alban Hills falling to the main forces of his Fifth Army driving up the Liri valley rather than to the VI Corps thrusting out from Anzio, diluted the second part of Lucas's mission by directing him to advance "on" the Alban Hills, not *to* them.

What Clark did in effect was what Moltke had done to Schlieffen's plan in World War I. In the same way that Moltke had weakened the right flank of the armies invading France, Clark had weakened his enveloping arm. The fact was, though Clark did not see it, that in the existing circumstances Clark could crack the Cassino line *only* if Lucas at Anzio was bold.

Whether Lucas was cautious or bold would depend in large measure on Lucas himself, on how he saw the situation confronting him at Anzio, on his judgment of his capabilities with respect to the German strength. On Lucas alone would rest the responsibility for the decision of what to do after he reached the shore at Anzio. Yet he had plenty of indications that Clark expected him to be prudent.

Contributing to General Lucas's uncertain frame of mind as he boarded ship for the voyage to Anzio was the progress of the big Fifth Army attack—the attack designed, at least, to pin the Germans down along the Cassino line but, ideally, to crack the line and get American troops into the Liri valley and headed for Frosinone and the Alban Hills.

General Clark had three corps facing the Cassino line. The British X Corps was on the left, deployed in the coastal zone along the Garigliano River. The U. S. II Corps was in the center on high ground overlooking the flooded Rapido River plain. One more hill mass, Mount Trocchio, remained to be taken before the II Corps could try to cross the Rapido. Once across, the corps would skirt the town of Cassino and the height on which perched the Abbey of Monte Cassino, then drive up the Liri River valley toward Frosinone and points north. On the right of the Fifth Army line was the French Expeditionary Corps of two French divisions, which had replaced the VI Corps in the mountains along the upper reaches of the Rapido.

The configuration of the terrain had these features: The

Liri River, flowing from the north, met and joined the Rapido, coming from the east. The juncture point was in front of the dominating hill mass of Monte Cassino. Both rivers then rushed to the sea in a single channel named the Garigliano.

Each corps of the Fifth Army thus confronted formidable obstacles. The British had to cross the fast-flowing and rather wide Garigliano, which was backed by high ground on the other side of the river. The Americans of the II Corps, after taking Mount Trocchio, had to cross the flooded Rapido River flats and the swift-flowing stream—both in the shadow of Monte Cassino—to get into the Liri valley. The French had to fight in a jumbled mass of mountain heights, some of the worst ground for combat in Italy.

The attack started on January 12 with the French. Despite the awful terrain and worse weather, they made a prodigious effort and gained several miles in three days, thereby pushing a dent in the Cassino line.

On January 15 the II Corps took Mount Trocchio, the last high ground on the near side of the Rapido River valley.

Two days later, on the 17th, the British attacked. Using DUKWs (amphibious trucks) and LCTs (landing craft, tank), British troops crossed the Garigliano not far from its mouth and wrested a slender bridgehead from the Germans on the other side of the river. The British quickly reinforced the bridgehead, and after two days the British held a piece of ground almost 4 miles deep, a serious breach of the Cassino line. Against stiffening resistance, the British tried to move north toward the Liri valley. But they could not enlarge their penetration.

On January 19 the X Corps launched another attack and tried to get troops across the Garigliano closer to the II Corps. This effort failed, as did another on the following day, the 20th.

On the evening of January 20 the II Corps sent the 36th Division toward the Rapido. If the division could get across and secure a foothold in the Liri valley, tanks that had been assembled behind would pass through the bridgehead and drive up the valley that Alexander considered the gateway to Rome.

The attack across the Rapido failed. Determined opposition, confusion among the assault troops, and plain bad luck conspired to turn a difficult river crossing into a near disaster. The 36th Division lost more than 1,000 men in a single night. The Liri valley remained closed.

Subsequent II Corps attacks also failed to gain the desired result, even though Americans managed to cross the Rapido farther upstream and threatened to take both the town of Cassino and the height of Monte Cassino. Despite continuing Fifth Army pressure, Clark failed to break the Cassino line that had been dented by the French, pierced by the British, and pushed in by the Americans. Immediate link-up with the Anzio force, if Lucas could get ashore and stay, was out of the question. Unless, of course, the threat posed by Lucas at Anzio was sufficient to prompt the Germans to withdraw from the Cassino line to meet the threat to Rome.

In a characteristic offhand remark, President Roosevelt once said that military planners were always conservative because they saw all the difficulties. Usually, he believed, more could be done than the planners were willing to admit.

The President was right. But his comment failed to take into account the tremendous complexity of warfare and the onerous burden carried by those who plan and execute it.

In World War II no military operation was more hazardous and complicated than an amphibious assault landing. None required more careful and painstaking preparation in every detail. Troops had to be selected, trained, and rehearsed. Men, baggage, vehicles, and supplies had to be made ready for shipment. Equipment had to be packed, crated, waterproofed, and marked for identification. All had to be moved to assembly areas, to points of embarkation, and finally loaded and stowed on vessels.

Space available aboard ships had to be matched with room needed. Manifests, troop lists, and loading tables had to be prepared. Key individuals and vital matériel had to be dispersed among several ships so that loss of any one vessel would not imperil the entire expedition.

Decisions had to be made on what to take, how soon it would be needed on the hostile shore, and where to put it aboard ship so that it could be unloaded in the desired order.

Throughout the whole process, men had to be fed and housed, equipment serviced, information disseminated, missions assigned, security and morale maintained.

Once aboard the vessels, the amphibious assault force had to be transported through hostile waters; landed on an enemy-held shore on the proper beach, in the proper order, at the proper time; supported and nourished despite opposition.

Not until the ground troops took their initial objectives and made the beachhead secure; not until men, weapons, and supplies could flow to the front in adequate quantities and without significant interruption could an amphibious assault be considered successfully completed.

Even then, more men, supplies, and equipment had to be brought across the water to build up the forces already ashore. Matériel had to be unloaded, segregated, and organized on the beach, then carried to inland dumps.

Planners had to count on ships allocated or promised, calculate the time needed to make the turnaround voyages between rear-area bases and the beach, try to employ suitable types of craft for a multitude of tasks, provide sufficient men to handle cargo on the beach, and be sure that a variety of equipment needed was available. They had to be sure the existing roads could handle the traffic or be prepared to build others to assure the flow of adequate supplies to the front without hindering the movement of troops and weapons and the evacuation of the wounded and injured.

Planners had to weigh the capabilities of their own forces against information about the enemy that came from such diverse intelligence sources as reports from agents, reconnaissance sorties, photographs, the interrogation of prisoners. They had to be certain that the assault troops would overcome the resistance that hostile forces could be expected to offer.

Over all these activities hovered certain specters, the incalculable factors of inclement weather, human fatigue, equipment breakdown, and enemy reaction.

To organize men, weapons, supplies, and equipment and embark them at Naples for a water movement of more than 100 miles designed to get them to their destination at an appointed time and in condition to overcome hostile forces, to manage the movement of sufficient follow-up troops and matériel to insure retention of the shore, to make the detailed arrangements for an amphibious operation to be executed by an assault force of some 30,000 men and 5,200 vehicles—about 27 infantry battalions—this was the task of the Anzio planners, a task that was further compounded by the short time available.

Rear Admiral Frank J. Lowry had the responsibility of embarking, landing, and supporting the Anzio force. His assault convoy numbered 2 command ships, 5 cruisers, 24 destroyers, 2 antiaircraft ships, 2 Dutch gunboats, 23 mine sweepers, 32 submarine chasers, 6 repair ships, 16 landing craft equipped with guns, antiaircraft weapons, and rockets, 4 Liberty ships, 8 LSIs (landing ships, infantry), 84 LSTs (landing ships, tank), 96 LCIs (landing craft, infantry), and 50 LCTs (landing craft, tank). These were divided into two task forces, one to carry and protect the American troops, the other the British.

Small naval parties were to precede the ground force assault waves to locate the beaches and mark them with colored lights. After daybreak, a naval salvage group was to lay ponton causeways to facilitate unloading.

Reinforced by elements of the British Desert Air Force, Major General Edwin J. House's U. S. XII Air Support Command would give direct support to the amphibious operation.

The ships of the assault convoy put out to sea from Naples early on January 21. Swinging south around Capri on a roundabout course to avoid German mine fields and to deceive the

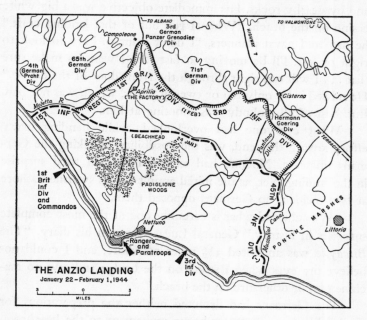

THE ANZIO LANDING
January 22 - February 1, 1944

Germans on their destination, the vessels turned sharply toward Anzio after nightfall.

At five minutes after midnight, the ships dropped anchor off Anzio. Assault craft were lowered into the water, patrol vessels herded them into formations, and shortly before 2 A.M., January 22, the boats were heading toward shore.

Ten minutes before two o'clock, two British landing craft equipped with rockets launched a five-minute barrage on the landing beaches, a deafening roar after the humming sound of the boats' motors.

There was no enemy reply. The shoreline in the Anzio area was dark and silent.

Everyone had expected the landing to be bitterly opposed. Colonel William O. Darby, who commanded the Ranger Force, for example, was concerned not only by the resistance he anticipated but also by the shallowness of the beach at Anzio and by nearby rocks. His immediate objective was a big white casino on the beach. "When I run out of that landing craft," he had told naval planners, "I don't want to have to look to right or left. I'll be moving so fast that I want to make sure that . . . I will run right through the front door of the casino." He missed it by only ten or twenty yards, which was not bad. But, best of all, nobody was shooting at him.

What everyone had overlooked, while bending every effort toward that end, was the possibility of taking the Germans unaware. No one had expected to gain total surprise in the landing. Yet, as the initial assault waves swarmed ashore at two o'clock, no Germans opposed them.

"We achieved what is certainly one of the most complete surprises in history," General Lucas wrote in his diary. "The *Biscayne* was anchored 3½ miles off shore, and I could not believe my eyes when I stood on the bridge and saw no machine gun or other fire on the beach."

The Germans had detected neither the preparations for the landing nor the water-borne movement to the beaches.

Allied planes flew more than 1,200 sorties on January 22 in direct support of the landing at Anzio, but they were not needed. The only resistance came from a few small coast artillery and antiaircraft units. Two batteries fired wildly for a few minutes before daylight until silenced by naval guns. A few other miscellaneous artillery pieces near the beaches had no chance even to open fire.

Small scattered mine fields, mostly in the port of Anzio, proved the greatest hazard to the troops coming ashore. The only opposition immediately inland came from two depleted coast-watching battalions recently relieved from the Cassino front for rest and rehabilitation, and they were quickly overrun.

The 3rd Division, landing on the beaches just south of Anzio, was 3 miles inland by midmorning, had all its artillery and tanks ashore, destroyed four bridges along the Mussolini Canal to protect its right flank, and then dug in to repel an expected German counterattack which did not materialize.

The three battalions of Rangers landed at Anzio and seized the port, while the 509th Parachute Infantry Battalion swung down the coastal road and occupied Nettuno, 2 miles away. Behind them came the 504th Parachute Infantry Regiment. "The day was sunny and warm," a paratrooper later remembered, "making it very hard to believe that a war was going on and that we were in the middle of it."

The British 1st Division, landing on beaches north of Anzio, was delayed somewhat by mines and shallow water, but, by midday, troops were more than 2 miles inland. British Commandos swung over to cut the road leading to Albano, and just north of Anzio they established a roadblock.

Behind the assault troops came engineers who cleared the scattered mine fields, bulldozed exit roads across the dunes, and handled streams of men and supplies coming ashore. Despite some sporadic long-range shelling from German guns inland and three hit-and-run raids by German planes, the beachhead was quickly organized. A mine sweeper was damaged by a mine, and an LCI was sunk by bombs, but engineers cleared the debris from the port of Anzio, naval personnel hauled away sunken vessels and swept the harbor, and by early afternoon the port of Anzio was ready to open in support of the beachhead. Because the British beaches were too shallow, Lucas closed them and switched British unloading operations to the newly opened port. By midnight of January 22, the VI Corps had about 36,000 men, 3,200 vehicles, and large quantities of supplies ashore—about 90 per cent of the equipment and personnel of the assault convoy.

Casualties were extremely light: 13 killed, 97 wounded, and 44 missing. The VI Corps had taken 227 prisoners.

With a beachhead firmly in hand and a port captured virtually intact, General Lucas was in an excellent position to attain the objectives that Generals Alexander and Clark, in their different ways, had set. Churchill, it seemed, had been right to pursue and fashion the strategic envelopment at Anzio. Thus far, at any rate, Anzio was a resounding success.

Three days before the invasion a second lieutenant in the German army, Leutnant Siegmund Seiler, arrived in Anzio. Forty years old, a mining engineer, and, according to his own description, "a civilian in uniform," he took charge of eighteen men. He was to make the port of Anzio useless by cutting two channels through the mole, thereby causing the harbor to sand up. He expected the job would take about three weeks.

Some time after nine o'clock on the evening of January 21, Seiler heard some explosions. They seemed to come from the town of Nettuno. His first thought was of an Allied invasion. He was relieved when he learned that an ammunition truck had driven into a roadblock on the outskirts of town. The ammunition had been set off by accident.

Still nervous an hour later, Seiler detected a persistent purring sound. He listened. It seemed to come from the sea. Could *this* be an Allied invasion?

He went to see the town commandant, a newly arrived officer like himself. Both officers listened. No question about it, Seiler said, the noise had gotten louder.

What could it be? Boats? It could only be something in connection with an enemy landing.

The town commandant had an idea. Not far away, on the

other side of Nettuno, a combat unit had established its headquarters. *They* would know if anything was wrong. Would
Seiler accompany him to the headquarters?

Seiler hesitated.

It would be well if he came, the town commandant explained, for in the event of an Allied landing, Seiler and his men
were to take their places in a defensive line that had been
planned.

Seiler was startled. He had never so much as seen an enemy
soldier. Was the town commandant sure about his having to
take part in combat?

No question about it. There was a secret order in the safe
that set forth the defensive positions. Seiler's detachment was
clearly marked for incorporation into the line.

Seiler agreed to accompany the town commandant.

By then it was after midnight. The humming was quite
loud. There was a rasp in the hum. No question about it, the
noise sounded like motors.

Taking a staff car and a sergeant to drive, the two officers
left Anzio, the town commandant sitting up front, Seiler in
the back. Inexplicably, they took the wrong road. By the time
they made their way to the coastal road between Anzio and
Nettuno, American troops were blocking the way.

When the sergeant tried to ram through the troops, the
Americans fired into the speeding car. Seiler considered them
"very substantial bursts."

The town commandant was killed, the sergeant wounded.
Seiler was safe. He had taken refuge behind the back seat,
where he had wedged himself deeply into a small recess.

The car came to a jarring halt in a ditch. In the sudden
silence, Seiler heard the door open. He raised his head. An
American soldier was motioning him to get out with his hands
up.

Seiler complied. He tried to hurry. It was difficult to get
out of the small space and his cramped position.

A doctor wearing the Red Cross stepped up and asked him whether he was hurt. He shook his head. Only shaken up and dazed. The coast road was crowded with American troops.

Taken under guard to the beach, where he would board a ship later for Naples and a prisoner of war camp, Seiler watched the landing operation. The smoothness of the work amazed him. He heard no words of command, yet everything went beautifully—"like clockwork," he said.

The beach was congested with matériel, and troops were moving around smartly, unloading, adjusting, correcting—"like a big market," Seiler said, "like a big business without confusion, disorder, or muddle."

The big amphibious vehicles and their ease of movement impressed him. But what struck him most of all was the maneuverability of the quarter-ton truck, the ubiquitous jeep, which he saw for the first time. "Like beetles," he said, "they helped each other out, pushing or pulling when stuck in the sand or water."

He could appreciate the careful planning that had gone into the operation when he noticed bulldozers working on the beach only a few hours after the first men had come ashore, grading the ground to make a road on which wire netting was placed "without loss of time."

He had a ringside seat to see American efficiency, and he marveled that "every man knew his place and his job."

Seiler watched the beach scene in fascination. No question about it—it was by far the most exciting day of his life. But what he could not get out of his mind was the sound of the humming motors in the boats bringing the troops ashore without interference.

How had the VI Corps taken the Germans so completely by surprise?

Having always considered the long sea flanks in Italy

cruelly exposed to Allied amphibious attacks, the Germans had drawn five plans to cope with the possibility of five such landings. They regarded a landing near Rome as the most serious threat.

If the Allies invaded the coast near Rome, Hitler planned to reinforce Kesselring with troops dispatched from France, the Balkans, and Germany. But since these reinforcements could hardly reach the landing area in time to be effective during the critical early hours, Kesselring himself was prepared to deal with a descent on the coast. Referring repeatedly to the principle that a commander without reserves could not influence the course of battle, Kesselring demanded that his subordinate commanders keep something in reserve, no matter how small. In accord with his own instruction, Kesselring constantly kept two divisions under his control in the Rome area. In January he had not only two divisions but also a parachute division he was organizing near by and a corps headquarters he could use to take tactical command of a defensive effort. Kesselring expected also to call upon Vietinghoff's Tenth Army in southern Italy for at least a division. He would draw upon the Fourteenth Army, which was charged with maintaining order in northern Italy, for one or two divisions. These would give him more than enough to repel an invasion.

The British crossing of the Garigliano on January 17 upset Kesselring's calculations. If the British enlarged their bridgehead and made a breakthrough into the Liri valley behind Cassino, they would fashion a threat that the Germans could not eliminate. With Cassino outflanked, the Germans would have to withdraw from their excellent positions along the Cassino line.

Vietinghoff, the Tenth Army commander, was quite explicit in his report. With the Allies exerting pressure all along the line, he did not have enough troops to stop the British. He needed at least two divisions to stabilize the situation. Could he have the two divisions stationed near Rome? Could he have them for just a few days? Once he re-established solid defensive positions, he would return the divisions to Kesselring's control.

"A bitter tussle," Kesselring's chief of staff, Siegfried Westphal, later recorded, "now began over the disposition of the two divisions." A difficult choice had to be made. Was the situation along the Garigliano really as critical as Vietinghoff thought? Even if it was, did that justify endangering the Rome area by transferring two divisions to the Tenth Army front?

Several days earlier the Germans had intercepted an Allied radio message that seemed to disclose the imminence of a landing. At that time Admiral Canaris, Chief of the Office of Foreign Intelligence in Berlin, happened to be visiting Kesselring's headquarters. When asked about the possibility of an amphibious assault, Canaris answered confidently. "At the present time," he said, "there is not the slightest sign that a new landing will be undertaken in the immediate future. The number of ships in the Naples harbor may be regarded as quite normal." Westphal passed the advice on to Vietinghoff. "I consider a large-scale landing operation," Westphal said quite categorically, "as being out of the question for the next four to six weeks."

Because of this estimate and because an Allied breakthrough to the Liri valley would make "the damage irreparable," Kesselring felt he could not refuse Vietinghoff's request for more troops. Since the Garigliano crossing was, in Kesselring's words, "the greatest crisis yet encountered," since the fate of the Tenth Army "hung by a slender thread," he yielded to Vietinghoff's urgent messages.

On January 18 Kesselring sent from the Rome area the two veteran divisions he had in reserve. To lighten Vietinghoff's task of controlling the divisions in battle, he also sent the I Parachute Corps headquarters. It was the arrival in increasing numbers on January 19 and 20 of these troops that prevented the British from expanding their Garigliano bridge-head.

But, as a consequence, the Rome area was virtually de-nuded of German troops. Kesselring had no forces available to counter Allied landings, no staff to organize even an emergency defense.

The Anzio landing, therefore, according to the first Ger-man estimate, had a good chance of bringing the Cassino line "to a state of collapse."

What Clark had hoped to achieve had more than come to pass. Not only had his massive three-corps attack pinned the Germans down along the Cassino line; it had also attracted Kesselring's reserves. The coast was clear for Lucas.

There was still another side to the coin. Attracting the additional German troops to the Cassino line had prevented the Fifth Army from getting into the Liri valley, either by way of the British bridgehead across the Garigliano or by way of the frontal entrance across the Rapido. If then the Fifth Army was stymied, it was up to Lucas to dislodge the opposition at Cassino by making good his threat in the German rear.

If Clark continued battering the Cassino line and if Lucas created a menace sufficient to scare the Germans, the situation for Kesselring was fraught with danger and difficulty. How could he erase the threat at Anzio while at the same time holding fast at Cassino?

An hour or so after the Allied troops began to land at Anzio, Kesselring learned of the invasion. But before he could take action, he had to know more about the landing. Was it a raid? Was it a feint to draw off his reserves? Or was it a landing in earnest?

Three hours after the landing the reports coming to Kes-selring told him what he needed to know. From the estimated size of the disembarking force, the Allies were making a large-scale invasion. From this, Kesselring guessed they would prob-ably try to seize the Alban Hills. If they did so, if they rapidly exploited their unopposed landing, they would jeopardize the entire German strategy of the Italian campaign.

At 5 A.M. Kesselring ordered the 4th Parachute Division, which was being activated just north of Rome, and some nearby replacement units of the Hermann Goering Division to block the roads leading from Anzio to the Alban Hills and to Rome.

At 6 A.M. Kesselring reported the landing to Hitler's headquarters and requested troops. The headquarters responded by ordering, later that day, the 715th Division to move from southern France to Italy, the 114th Division from the Balkans, miscellaneous units in about division strength from Germany; and by authorizing the activation of a new division in northern Italy—the 92nd—to be formed from several replacement battalions.

At 7:10 Kesselring ordered the Fourteenth Army to make forces available. This army ordered the 65th Division (less one regiment) at Genoa, the 362nd Division (less one regiment) at Rimini, and some elements of the newly formed 16th SS Panzer Grenadier Division at Leghorn to proceed immediately to Anzio. These units started to move that evening.

At 8:30 A.M., reluctantly, for Kesselring appreciated how difficult Vietinghoff's situation was, Kesselring directed the Tenth Army to transfer from the Cassino line a corps headquarters and all the combat troops that could be spared. In compliance, Vietinghoff designated the I Parachute Corps headquarters (which had recently arrived from the Rome area), the 3rd Panzer Grenadier Division (less one regiment), the 71st Division, and parts of the Hermann Goering Division for movement. These began to march toward Anzio the same day. Not long afterward would go the 26th Panzer Division and elements of the 1st Parachute Division from the Adriatic side of the Tenth Army front.

Some time during the morning Kesselring instructed the Commandant of Rome, the only general officer available, to

take over, with an improvised staff, command of the Anzio
front until the arrival of the I Parachute Corps headquarters.

With these events set into motion, there was nothing more
for Kesselring to do but to wait for Lucas to show his hand.

German troops were meanwhile hurrying toward Anzio.
At 5 P.M. the I Parachute Corps headquarters took command
of the Anzio sector and hustled the miscellaneous battalions as
they arrived into a precarious defensive line around the Allied
beachhead.

The battle lines were drawn, and by the evening of January 22, the Germans were feeling a small measure of confidence. Allied behavior at the scene of the landing reassured
them. According to one report:

> The Allies on the beachhead on the first day of the landing
> did not conform to the German High Command's expectations.
> Instead of moving northward with the first wave to seize the
> Alban Mountains . . . the landing forces limited their objective.
> Their initial action was to occupy a small beachhead. . . . As the
> Allied forces made no preparations for a large-scale attack on the
> first day of the landings, the German Command estimated that
> the Allies would improve their positions, and bring up more
> troops. . . . During this time, sufficient German troops would
> arrive to prevent an Allied breakthrough.

This expression of confidence was perhaps nothing more
than whistling in the dark, for Westphal remarked a "state of
acute continuous tension" at Kesselring's headquarters. Yet
Kesselring himself was optimistic. Optimism was his trade
mark. But he sincerely felt that he had a good chance of re-
covering from the setback the surprising landing at Anzio
represented. The lack of aggressiveness on the part of the VI
Corps, Kesselring decided, would permit him to fashion a successful defense.

On the Cassino line, in contrast, the situation was fraught
with anxiety. Vietinghoff telephoned that evening to advocate

immediate withdrawal in order to eliminate the Anzio beach-head. How could he hold at Cassino when so many troops had been pulled out of the line?

Kesselring told him to hold fast. There would be no with-drawal from Cassino.

This was a courageous decision. The first strong German contingents could not arrive at Anzio before January 24. If the Allies launched an attack on January 23 or 24, they would overrun, Kesselring estimated, the few German forces that opposed them. In effect, the road to the Alban Hills was open. Beyond the Alban Hills, Rome lay virtually undefended.

THE ATTACK

5 ON THE SECOND DAY of the invasion, January 23, the Anzio force slightly increased the size of the beachhead. The only real progress was at the shoreline, where more troops came ashore, more equipment and supplies were unloaded.

Kesselring could sigh in relief that evening. He could tell Vietinghoff, the Tenth Army commander, he "believed that the danger of a large-scale expansion of the beachhead was no longer imminent."

The next day was also uneventful, except for gale winds and high surf, which brought unloading operations to a halt. The 1st British Division moved to the Moletta River, a good anchor for the left flank of the beachhead. The U. S. 3rd Division, plus the Rangers and the 504th Parachute Infantry, took several additional bridges along the Mussolini Canal to make the right flank more secure. The beachhead was 7 miles deep, the front was 16 miles in length, and in compliance with instructions, Lucas was holding large forces in reserve in anticipation of a German counterattack.

This pattern pleased Kesselring. As one report noted: "The Allied landing forces limited themselves to reconnaissance and patrol. . . . By this time, the German defenses had been strongly reinforced, and the German Command considered the danger of an Allied breakthrough to be removed." By restricting his forces to the task of consolidating the beachhead, Lucas restrained his efforts to local attacks, and these, the Germans felt, they could handle.

"On January 22 and even the following day," Westphal later wrote, "an audacious and enterprising formation of enemy troops . . . could have penetrated into the city of Rome itself without having to overcome any serious opposition. . . . But the landed enemy forces lost time and hesitated." And this gave the German countermeasures a good chance to succeed.

Alexander and Clark had visited Anzio on January 22—D Day—and both were satisfied. Though Alexander was very optimistic, Clark was somewhat subdued, for he was depressed by the failure of the large-scale attack on his main front to break through the Cassino line and get into the Liri valley.

"The last thing Clark said to me on D-Day before he embarked for [the return trip to] Naples," General Lucas later remembered, "was 'Don't stick your neck out, Johnny. I did at Salerno and got into trouble.' "

Lucas was not about to stick his neck out. Having gained surprise in his landing, he proceeded to disregard the advantage it gave him. Two days after coming ashore, he was still only contemplating a push out from the beachhead. He knew what he ought to do. "I must keep in motion," he wrote in his diary, "if my first success is to be of any value." But his outward pressure was by no means an all-out drive toward the Alban Hills.

What interested Lucas more was building up his beachhead. He had captured the Anzio harbor intact, he had put it into operation immediately to handle incoming troops and supplies, and this was, he felt, quite an achievement. The port was his "salvation," he said, for it kept him tied to the Fifth Army and its supplies of men, weapons, and equipment. To keep his supply line intact, Lucas gave his personal attention to setting up an antiaircraft warning system, to building an airfield, to clearing the clutter of supplies and equipment that jammed the beachhead behind the first row of dunes.

Lucas's concern with the logistics of the landing came not only from Clark's and Brann's suggestions of caution but also from his own natural prudence. Besides, he was apprehensive because he believed that the Germans could increase their build-up overland faster than he could by water transport. He feared that the Germans might attack before he could cut their lines of communication. When his intelligence officers informed him that the Germans were taking troops from the Cassino line to oppose him at Anzio, he was hardly reassured. While a weakened Cassino line might permit the Fifth Army to advance toward Rome, powerful German rearguards in the Liri valley, he was sure, would retard Allied progress. Seeing no possibility of a swift drive up the Liri, Lucas expected his force to be consigned to at least temporary isolation. Thus his primary concern was building up his strength. "The strain of a thing like this is a terrible burden," he confessed. "Who the hell wants to be a general?"

"My days are filled with excitement and anxiety," Lucas wrote on January 25, the fourth day of the invasion, "although I feel now that the beachhead is safe and I can plan for the future with some assurance." A regiment of the 45th Division was coming ashore that day, and Lucas awaited the arrival of most of the 1st Armored Division and the remainder of the 45th. "That is about all I can supply but I think it will be enough." Meanwhile, the 1st British and 3rd U. S. Divisions were advancing "to extend the beachhead a little."

Actually, while the American division was having tough going trying to advance northeast toward Cisterna, the British division was making a surprisingly easy advance northward along the road toward Albano. From the German viewpoint, loss of Cisterna would cut Highway 7 and open the way to Valmontone astride Highway 6, a distinct threat to the Tenth Army. Though Albano gave access to Rome, Kesselring by this time was sure that Lucas was too cautious to streak into the Eternal City.

The British moved 4 miles on January 25 along the Albano road toward Campoleone and captured Aprilia, called the "Factory," along with 111 prisoners. Campoleone and Cisterna, obvious jump-off points for an advance on the Alban Hills, were then less than 4 miles ahead of the British and American troops, respectively. But Lucas was not yet ready to move. Nor was he about to hurry. "I must keep my feet on the ground and my forces in hand," he wrote in his diary, "and do nothing foolish. This is the most important thing I have ever tried to do and I will not be stampeded."

Clark, in the meantime, had concluded that the Germans would not pull out of Cassino because of the threat at Anzio. He figured they would gather strong forces from other sources and counterattack the beachhead. Thus Lucas had to be careful. But Lucas also had to be aggressive. Lucas had to take some chances too.

When Clark visited Lucas on January 25, he was impressed by Lucas's logistical arrangements. What worried him, he confided to Lucas, were the developments on the Cassino front, "where," Lucas noted, "the bloodiest fight of the war is in progress." The Cassino battle, Lucas wrote, could "not be resolved I am afraid until I can get my feet under me and make some further progress." In other words, only if Lucas made a powerful threat toward the Alban Hills would the Germans relax their pressure at Cassino. Yet still he refused to hurry. "I am doing my best but it seems terribly slow."

Lucas was waiting for more troops, which Clark, expecting a crushing counterblow, was planning to send.

Alexander also paid Lucas a visit on the 25th and complimented him. "What a splendid piece of work," Alexander said.

Lucas reminded him that the task was not yet finished.

Still, Lucas did have a beachhead nearly 10 miles deep, not bad, Lucas thought, for the fourth day of the invasion. "I must hold it," he wrote in his diary, "and think I can."

Rain, hail, and sleet came on January 26 to disrupt the supply build-up. "This waiting is terrible," Lucas wrote. "I want an all-out Corps effort but the time hasn't come yet and the weather will not help matters. Bad for tanks. . . . I hope to get moving soon. Must move before the enemy build-up gets too great."

He might be able to attack, he thought, in a few days. But he was determined to have the entire 45th Division at Anzio before he launched his all-out effort.

Two heavy air raids that night did considerable damage, destroying trucks and ammunition dumps, killing a number of men, starting fires, gouging big craters in the roads. But the port was still operating, the ships were unloading, "thank God."

Calling his division commanders to a meeting on January 27, Lucas talked over plans for the future. This made him feel better about the prospects of launching a strong attack out of the beachhead. Not only did his subordinate commanders cheer him, but the news about incoming ships was good. He expected thirty LSTs to be unloaded at Anzio that day as compared with seven the day before, and he thought that thirty more could be unloaded on the following day.

By this time the 3rd Division had pushed to within 3 miles of Cisterna, the British had repulsed a counterattack at Aprilia (the Factory), destroying four German tanks and a self-propelled gun and capturing 46 prisoners. With the Factory well in hand, the British were ready to attack Campoleone. Yet Lucas still waited.

On that day, January 27, Alexander was expressing dissatisfaction to Clark over the way Lucas was running things. Lucas, Alexander believed, was pushing neither rapidly enough nor hard enough.

Though Clark himself had vaguely felt that progress was lagging at Anzio, he had been too busy at the Cassino front to do more than recognize the nagging doubt. Prodded by the talk with Alexander, he decided to go to Anzio the next day to see the situation for himself. But at the same time he resented

Alexander's words because he sensed Churchill's hot breath in the conversation. The Prime Minister, Clark thought, was trying to run the battle from London, and Churchill wanted an attack, Rome, and a victory no matter how many tactical or logistical reasons argued against them.

At Anzio on January 28, Clark found the situation far from clear. Though he appreciated Lucas's thoroughness, though he recognized that the final outcome of the struggle depended on which side could increase its forces more quickly, he urged Lucas to take bold offensive action. What he had in mind was taking Cisterna and Campoleone, which would give Lucas key points for a strong defensive line.

This was not what Lucas understood. Stung by Clark's comments, Lucas felt obliged that evening to explain his entire course of action. In his diary, he wrote:

Apparently some of the higher levels think I have not advanced with maximum speed. I think more has been accomplished than anyone had a right to expect. This venture was always a desperate one and I could never see much chance for it to succeed, if success means driving the Germans north of Rome. The one factor that has allowed us to get established ashore has been the port of Anzio. Without it our situation by this time would have been desperate with little chance of a build-up to adequate strength. As it is, we are doing well and, in addition to troops, unloaded over 4,000 tons of supplies yesterday.

Had I been able to rush to the high ground around Albano . . . immediately upon landing, nothing would have been accomplished except to weaken my force by that amount because the troops sent, being completely beyond supporting distance, would have been immediately destroyed. The only thing to do was what I did. Get a proper beachhead and prepare to hold it. Keep the enemy off balance by a constant advance against him by small units, not committing anything as large as a division until the Corps was ashore and everything was set. Then make a coordinated attack to defeat the enemy and seize the objective. Follow this by exploitation.

This is what I have been doing but I had to have troops in to do it with.

The fact that Clark announced his intention of staying at Anzio perhaps for several days also disturbed Lucas. Conscious that Clark had been somewhat harsh with him, Lucas did not know that the Fifth Army commander had previously defended Lucas's course of action to Alexander.

Again Lucas wrote in his diary:

His [Clark's] gloomy attitude is certainly bad for me. He thinks I should have been more aggressive on D-Day and should have gotten tanks and things out to the front. I think he realizes the serious nature of the whole operation. His forces are divided in the face of a superior enemy on interior lines and now neither of the parts is capable of inflicting a real defeat on those facing it. There has been no chance, with available shipping, to build "Shingle" up to a decisive strength and anyone with any knowledge of logistics could have seen that from the start. I have done what I was ordered to do, desperate though it was. I can win if I am let alone but I don't know whether I can stand the strain of having so many people looking over my shoulder. We must continue to push the Germans.

The basic fact was, nonetheless, that Lucas had not pushed the Germans much. As a German general later summed it up:

Every minute was precious for the Germans and Allies alike. What would have happened if the enemy had advanced boldly immediately after landing, if he had occupied the Alban Mountains and thrust on to Valmontone, thereby cutting off the vital supply roads of . . . the Tenth Army? But the enemy did not make this advance, he did not feel strong enough; thus he threw away his great chance. This neglect was an error. . . . The enemy's methodical, playing-for-safety manner of waging war was revealed again in the first days of the fighting for the beachhead. He felt his way forward cautiously to the northeast towards Cisterna, and northwards in the direction of Aprilia-Campoleone . . . it was already too late.

On January 29, the eighth day of the invasion, Lucas at last felt strong enough to make his offensive bid. He would strike hard with three divisions on the following day. But by this time Kesselring, too, was ready.

From northern Italy, southern Italy, Germany, France, and Yugoslavia, German units had moved toward Anzio. No time had been lost in setting the transfers into motion. Despite Allied air attacks against roads and railways, the Germans were little harried. They moved at night, and strict regulation and good organization, plus the availability of Italian trucks, made it possible to bring up the troops in much less time than the Allies had believed feasible.

So rapidly did the German build-up develop that Kesselring, who had set the mad race into motion, found time now to slow the pace. The 715th Division, for example, ordered originally to proceed from Avignon, France, without interruption day and night, regardless of traffic conditions and without thought of wear and tear on vehicles, now received advice from Kesselring's headquarters to exercise normal care. There was no point in having at Anzio an exhausted division that would need a week or so to get ready for battle.

The first reinforcements arrived from southern Italy—parts and pieces of the 3rd and 29th Panzer Grenadier, 71st, and Hermann Goering Divisions—as early as January 22. Four days later the first units from northern Italy—advance elements of the 65th and 362nd Divisions—began to reach the Rome area.

Despite immense energy and resolution, it took time to put even scanty German forces into action on the front. The immediate task was to erect and organize a defensive line from the "jumble of multifarious troops," as one German general put it, "which streamed in from all directions." Though the Germans disliked breaking up established formations, they could not avoid it, and "oddly assorted groups succeeded in combining together to organize the first significant defense against the enemy landing." Restoring the normal chain of command had to be postponed. But since "no attack aimed at gaining possession of the Alban Mountains had been launched by the enemy on 23 or 24 January," the German general concluded, "the first and greatest crisis had been overcome."

Convinced that the threat to the Alban Hills was averted for the time being and that the acute danger of an Allied breakthrough north to Rome or northeast to Valmontone had passed, Kesselring made use of a further breathing spell to consolidate positions and bring some order into the confused mass of heterogeneous units at the beachhead. He also ordered Vietinghoff once again to hold firm at Cassino, though he relented to the extent of authorizing slow and gradual withdrawal, if absolutely necessary, on the Adriatic front.

At Anzio, Kesselring set himself three tasks. He had to prevent further enlargement of the Allied beachhead, he had to compress the beachhead area, and he had to launch an attack to push the Allies into the sea. The beachhead had to be eliminated quickly, for Vietinghoff could not do indefinitely without the forces his Tenth Army had released. Hitler also made it clear that the reinforcements Kesselring was in the process of receiving from other theaters were only temporary. As soon as the beachhead was destroyed, a number of units would have to be sent to France to oppose the Allied attack across the Channel expected in the spring.

Since the forces on both sides of the beachhead were rapidly increasing their strength, Kesselring on January 24 ordered the Fourteenth Army headquarters to move from Verona in Northern Italy to take command from the I Parachute Corps. When the army commander, General Eberhard von Mackensen, assumed control on the following day, he had elements of eight divisions deployed along a defensive line around the beachhead, elements of five more on their way.

Mackensen's primary mission, Kesselring announced, was

to launch a decisive counterattack. This he hoped Mackensen could execute as early as the 28th. But on second thought, Kesselring himself, despite instructions from Hitler to counterattack as soon as possible, postponed Mackensen's attack until February 1 when additional troops would be available.

Like Churchill vitally interested in Anzio, Hitler concerned himself with all aspects of Kesselring's problems, even going so far as to check minor tactical details. He constantly stressed the importance of the impending battle. Not only was Kesselring fighting a battle for Rome, not only was the outcome to determine the fate of the Tenth Army in southern Italy; the battle, Hitler believed, transcended the entire Italian theater and would affect the final verdict of the war.

Immensely concerned with Anzio from the first day of the invasion, Hitler had personally asked Goering to make available transport planes to move troops to the beachhead, a task that Goering could not fulfill. Hitler then insisted on air attacks against Allied ships in an effort to cut the beachhead from its source of supplies.

The *Luftwaffe* harassed the Allies constantly. Fighter-bombers attacked the beachhead every few hours, medium bombers struck periodically, launching in addition to conventional bombs torpedoes and radio-controlled "glider" bombs. Three major air raids on January 23, 24, and 26 sank a British destroyer and a hospital ship, damaged another hospital ship, and drove a Liberty ship ashore; three days later, the *Luftwaffe* sank a Liberty ship and a British antiaircraft cruiser.

Yet the attacks cost the Germans dearly. During the first week of the invasion, the Germans lost almost a hundred planes to the Allied air defenses of 40-mm. and 90-mm. antiaircraft guns. Allied barrage balloons moored to the ships prevented low-level bombing, and extensive smoke screens masked the beachhead.

German floating mines sank an LST and an LCI with the

loss of three hundred men, and long-range artillery pieces shelled both the troops working the beaches and the ships off-shore. But all these, even the air strikes, were in reality no more than nuisance weapons. The decisive punch would have to come from a ground attack.

Mackensen, the Fourteenth Army commander, divided his defensive line into three sectors—the Hermann Goering Division in the eastern part defending Cisterna, the 3rd Panzer Grenadier Division in the center defending Campoleone, the 65th Division in the west behind the Moletta River. But these dispositions were clearer on a map than they were in actuality on the ground. Units were still inextricably mixed along the front.

On January 28, Kesselring submitted to Hitler Mackensen's plan for the counterattack scheduled for February 1, but on the following day Kesselring postponed the attack again, this time until the 2nd. For Hitler had reported "reliable information" of a second projected landing at Civitavecchia, fifty miles above Rome. Though the intensity of the continuing battle at Cassino and the size of the Allied beachhead force argued against a second landing, Kesselring had to divert some troops to Civitavecchia just in case the invasion really came.

For the attack on February 2, Kesselring would have Mackensen strike along the entire front, with a main effort down the road from Albano to Anzio. But while they were preparing this offensive, Lucas, on January 30, launched his own all-out attack.

The large coastal plain between the Anzio beaches and the Alban Hills was formerly the pestilential Pontine Marshes. A fertile farming region in Roman times, later neglected until it became a vast malarial swamp, the area had been reclaimed in part by the Fascist government by means of a complex grid of drainage canals and ditches. The largest waterway, almost in the center of the plain and used by Lucas to protect his right flank, was the Mussolini Canal, 240 feet wide from the top of one embankment to the other, the water between the smooth sloping banks 10 to 20 feet deep. South of the Mussolini Canal the Germans had flooded the ground as a defensive measure. There, except for a few roads along the tops of dikes, so straight as to be startling, so open and exposed as to be frightening, the terrain had reverted to its primitive state, a virtually impassable marsh.

From Terracina on the southern edge of the coastal plain, Highway 7 runs for 30 miles in an undeviating line to Cisterna at the foot of the Alban Hills, a railway paralleling the road for much of the way. From Cisterna, 30 miles from Rome, Highway 7 climbs into the Alban foothills, swings across the western slope, and reaches Albano, less than 15 miles below Rome. Twenty miles northeast of Cisterna is Valmontone. Sitting astride Highway 6, which passes around the eastern side of the Alban Hills, Valmontone is at the upper end of the Liri valley.

A great volcano, long since dormant, had formed the Alban Hills. Inside the rim of the crater, which has a diameter of 8 miles, are two large lakes, many fertile fields, and several wooded hills. From the two highest hills, rising hundreds of feet above the crater floor, the Germans had unrestricted observation over the Allied beachhead.

Lying directly ahead of the Allied troops was a vast expanse of farmland, slightly rolling, interlaced with irrigation ditches, and dotted with stone and masonry farmhouses. The main road out of the beachhead ran north up a gradual slope from Anzio to Albano and Highway 7. Dirt roads led to Cisterna and beyond to Valmontone.

If General Lucas could take both Albano and Valmontone, he would cut both main highways connecting the German Tenth Army in southern Italy with Rome. Not only would he block the escape routes of the forces fighting at Cassino; he would also be at the gates of the Eternal City.

The attack Lucas planned for January 30 called for extensive naval, air, and artillery support of a two-pronged ground advance with the main blow on the left. The British 1st Division was to take the Albano road to the top of the high ground, while the 1st U. S. Armored Division swung wide around the British left to come in on the hills from the west. On the right the 3rd U. S. Division, with the 504th Parachute Regiment and the Ranger Force under its command, was to advance to Cisterna, cut Highway 7, and be ready to drive on Valmontone and thrust against the Alban Hills from the east.

Because the two prongs of the attack would diverge, Lucas insisted on keeping tight control. He designated specific phase lines, beyond which advances could not be made without his approval. For he did not want his forces to run unchecked and become overextended, thereby giving the Germans an opportunity to split the Allied forces down the middle.

To spearhead the 3rd Division attack on Cisterna, two of the three Ranger battalions were to infiltrate during the night into the town, the third battalion meanwhile clearing the road for tanks and other reinforcements to be rushed forward the next morning to block Highway 7 in strength.

Getting ready on the evening of January 29, T/5 James P. O'Reilly—Technician Fifth Grade (Corporal)—along with other men of the 1st and 3rd Ranger Battalions, stripped his pack to essentials and rations. He discarded his tracer bullets, usual procedure for night operations, and stuffed extra hand grenades into his pockets. He stacked his bedroll and personal belongings at the company supply tent, these to be brought to Cisterna the following day along with supplies. Though mail had arrived that day, there was no time for distribution to the companies that evening. In Cisterna, the mail clerk promised, in the morning. He would bring up the letters the next day.

With two bandoleers of ammunition across their shoulders, the men slipped across the west branch of the Mussolini Canal at one-thirty on the morning of January 30 and in one long

column crept silently along a large, half-dry irrigation canal
called the Pantano ditch. The night was dark, the weather bitterly cold. Moving past German positions, the men hugged
the sides of the ditch as German sentries walked along the
banks. It was quiet. Not even the customary artillery or the
familiar burp of machine pistols sounded. Yet there were
enough small noises to indicate the presence of enemy troops
all around. The men were tense, half expecting at any moment
the violent eruption of sound that would signal the start of
battle.

Walking along the bottom of the ditch in knee-deep
water, O'Reilly kept thinking of the mail that had arrived.
What a lousy thing, no time for mail call. It was too damn
quiet. The water in the ditch was cold. But the mail would be
up in the morning.

The two Ranger battalions were still moving when the
thin line of dawn edged the horizon. The head of the 1st Battalion leading the column was less than half a mile from
Cisterna; the tail of the 3rd Battalion at the other end of the
column was about a mile and a half to the rear.

As the troops left the ditch to deploy for attack into
Cisterna, the noise they had all been awaiting and hoping
against suddenly exploded and passed through them with a
rush. German fire came in from all sides. They had been am-
bushed.

Though taken by surprise, the Rangers fought back. They
knew what to do and were pretty good at it. But they had little
cover and only light weapons. They were no match for the
machine guns, mortars, and tanks that threw a flaming wall
of fire at them. One battalion commander was killed almost
immediately, the other was severely wounded. With many
subordinate leaders knocked out as casualties, the Rangers
broke into small groups of varying effectiveness, continuing to
fight from the irrigation ditches in the hope that help would
come from the rear.

O'Reilly found himself walking toward a small vineyard where small puffs of greyish smoke were growing. What a lousy thing for a vineyard to have, a Kraut machine gun. He could finally hear it, distinguish through the furious noises around him the low cough of the weapon. He fell to his knees and started crawling up a ditch. He got up and ran the last few yards, almost falling on two neatly camouflaged German soldiers. They were changing their ammunition clips, and O'Reilly was able to shoot them both before they could get their gun into action. He did it without even thinking. It just came naturally. Later, when he thought about it, he was surprised at how natural it had been.

On the outskirts of Cisterna during the middle of the morning, a column of armored vehicles approached from the rear. The Rangers, almost out of ammunition by then, cheered in welcome and started to come out of the ditches.

The tanks and self-propelled guns were German. They cut down the Americans, shot them out of the irrigation canals, blew them to pieces.

Using captured Rangers as hostages, the Germans walked them up and down the roads, trying in that way to persuade other Rangers to surrender, promising to shoot the prisoners if the others refused. A German officer, O'Reilly remembered, kept yelling the same sentence over and over again in perfect English: "Come out or your comrades die." Most of the Rangers, about 500 of them, eventually came out of the ditches and surrendered. The rest were seriously wounded or dead.

O'Reilly worked his way carefully to the rear. The only mail that would be delivered in Cisterna that day would be German letters. But back in the company area, if he could get back, O'Reilly was sure he had some letters waiting for him.

He did not make it. There were too many Germans too near. He had to give up. . . .

At the Ranger Force headquarters, Colonel Darby was close to his radio and close to tears. He was heartsick and helpless. These were his men who were being annihilated. He had helped form the first Ranger battalion in North Ireland two years earlier. (Had it been only two years ago?) He had been the first commanding officer of the battalion. He had raised the men, transformed them into his image of the tough and resourceful Ranger. He had brought them ashore in North Africa. He had organized two more battalions, fought with them in Sicily, then in Italy. Was he to lose them at Cisterna?

He exhorted the 4th Ranger Battalion to get up to the encircled troops. He pleaded with the 3rd Division commander to get some troops up to Cisterna. He had to be restrained almost forcibly from going up to join his men.

The situation was hopeless. Despite herculean efforts, nobody could break through to the surrounded Rangers. The Hermann Goering Division, fighting from dug-in and well-organized positions, heavily supported by artillery and tanks, was too strong. But what had made it patently impossible for the Americans to budge the Hermann Goerings was the arrival that morning of the first elements of the 715th Division coming from southern France. Mackensen fed these troops into the Cisterna defenses as they arrived.

By noontime it was over. Of the 767 Rangers who had started toward Cisterna, only 6 returned.

The 3rd Division attack lasted for three days, from January 30 through February 1. After advancing two or three miles up the country roads leading to Cisterna, the division was stopped cold, unable to break through the Germans defending the last mile into town. Not only were units of the Hermann Goering and 715th Division opposing the Americans on the last day, but parts of the 26th Panzer Division, arriving at full speed from the Adriatic side of the Tenth Army line, had added their weight to the defenses.

Of all the attacking units of the 3rd Division, the 1st Battalion of the 7th Infantry had the most success. According to an account by Lieutenant Nicholas J. Grunzweig, a platoon leader in that battalion, this is what happened.

With the mission to cut Highway 7 just above Cisterna, the battalion faced unbelievably open terrain, very gently rolling fields reaching toward Cisterna, with stone farmhouses neatly spaced about 800 yards apart along rural lanes. Aerial photographs showed no obstacles, but what had appeared to be small hedges turned out to be deep ditches covered with brush. The battalion had little knowledge of the enemy strength and dispositions but, expecting a strictly defensive attitude on the part of the Germans, planned to advance by means of a night infiltration attack march—the troops to knife through the opposition at a rapid rate with the entire force in close column to facilitate control.

At 2 A.M. on January 30, half an hour after the Rangers jumped off, the battalion moved silently across its line of departure, the scouts following the compass needle due north. Almost immediately a farmhouse area with wire fences blocked the way and forced the battalion to split into small groups. Then a ditch 25 feet deep dispersed the troops still further. An explosion sounded in the rear and a huge fire flamed in Anzio about this time. The fire helped the men to see, but it also silhouetted them to the Germans. When a machine pistol up ahead expectorated a livid burst of fire, the battalion halted while a platoon deployed to engage the weapon, apparently an outpost position. The German gunner withdrew, firing as he went.

At daylight the battalion was moving across an extremely flat piece of ground about the size of a football field, with low rises on both sides and to the front, when a German flare appeared. A moment later machine guns opened fire, driving the Americans to cover. The troops scattered, some throwing themselves into ditches, others storming up a small hill to the protection of a slight defile.

Though the first bursts of German fire killed or wounded many men, small groups began to organize defensive positions.

There the battalion remained all day, the men under fire and suffering increasing losses. The battalion commander called repeatedly for tanks and tank destroyers to come up in support, but the vehicles could not get across the ditches. By evening each rifle company was down to about seventy men, but the battalion continued to hold through the night.

American tanks finally appeared at daybreak. Fatigued after thirty hours under German fire, the men nevertheless felt pretty good to have the tanks near by. When the regimental commander ordered the attack resumed at 2 P.M., the men genuinely felt they could move ahead and cut Highway 7.

Preparatory artillery fire plastered the German positions in tremendous volume. As the men of the battalion listened to the shelling, a sudden, driving determination that was close to anger seized them. Despite heavy German fire, they advanced almost a mile to burst into German positions in an orchard. The Germans fled, but encumbered by heavy overcoats, they made excellent targets.

The battalion pushed on to the railroad embankment, almost to the highway, but there the momentum of the attack stalled. German fire was heavy, and the tanks could not cross the embankment to take out the enemy weapons.

Reduced to a handful of troops, low on ammunition, fatigued from the endless fighting, what remained of the battalion dug in for the night. As the last shreds of daylight streaked the sky, the assistant division commander came forward and ordered the men to pull back. Their surge through the orchard had gained only an exposed salient vulnerable to counterattack, a piece of ground jutting far out in front of adjacent troops. This terrain, higher headquarters judged, the battalion was too weak to defend.

The battalion withdrew. What it had taken from the Germans it gave back. Of the 800 men who had launched the attack, only 150 remained.

Attacking toward Albano on the other side of the beach-head, the 1st British Division made better progress. After three days of attack the British held Campoleone and in the process had pierced Kesselring's main line of resistance.

In contrast, the 1st U. S. Armored Division found it impossible to advance because of rough stream gullies, muddy fields, and lack of cover. The tanks bogged down, stumbled over obstacles, pitched into ditches, as the men fought and cursed the terrain. The Italian farmhouses also posed a serious problem. Heavy stone construction made each building a fortification that had to be reduced by a small separate operation.

From General Lucas's point of view, soon after the attack jumped off, the corps had become "engaged in a hell of a struggle." As far as he was concerned, "There is never a big breakthrough except in story books. . . . The situation, from where I sit, is crowded with doubt and uncertainty. I expect to be counterattacked in some force, maybe considerable force, tomorrow morning."

General Clark was still at Anzio on the last day of January. "I don't blame him for being terribly disappointed," Lucas wrote. "He and those above him thought this landing would shake the Cassino line loose at once but they had no right to think that, because the German is strong in Italy and will give up no ground if he can help it."

What neither commander knew was how close the Allies actually had come to breaking out of the beachhead. The Germans stopped the VI Corps attack, but only with the greatest effort and with extremely high losses. Like the Allies, the Germans suffered casualties of about 5,500 men. Not only did Kesselring have to postpone Mackensen's offensive, but he had to permit the troops to go over entirely on the defensive. Desperately juggling their forces and employing all their reserves, the Germans just managed to hold.

What appeared to the Allies like overwhelming strength was what Kesselring called "a higgledy-piggledy jumble—

units of numerous divisions fighting confusedly side by side."
Because Allied intelligence officers identified many different
division units, they had to assume, in the absence of information to the contrary, that each division was present in its entirety. Total troops then, like total units, they guessed, far
outnumbered the VI Corps. Yet in actuality, the Allies had
about 100,000 men at Anzio, the Germans less than 90,000.

Despite the virtual equality in numbers, the Allies had
the advantage of fighting with balanced forces. The amphibious operation had been carefully planned and prepared,
whereas the German countermeasures were taken on the spur
of the moment. In a period of stress and emergency, the Germans had hastily assembled what was available and hurriedly
established defenses. For the most part, fragments, remnants,
and splinters of divisions, depleted units, recently organized
units, provisional commands, barely trained troops manned the
line. From the German point of view, the defensive stand was
nothing short of miraculous.

General Alexander arrived at Anzio on February 1 and
consulted with Clark and Lucas. According to Lucas, Alexander was

. . . kind enough but I am afraid he is not pleased. My head will
probably fall in the basket but I have done my best. There were
just too many Germans here for me to lick and they could build
up faster than I could. As I told Clark yesterday, I was sent on a
desperate mission, one where the odds were greatly against success, and I went without saying anything because I was given an
order and my opinion was not asked. The condition in which I
find myself is much better than I ever anticipated or had any
right to expect.

When Alexander and Clark departed from Anzio, Lucas
felt reassured. He had expected they had come to relieve him
of command. Instead, Clark apologized for having harassed
Lucas as much as he had—"I am glad he did," Lucas wrote, "as
I really like him very much." But best of all, Alexander and

Clark had seen the desperate nature of the fighting and could appreciate the speed of the German build-up. And Lucas was pleased and proud to have shown them the port and the beaches working at capacity. Stocks of supplies at the beachhead were at least ten days ahead of schedule.

So favorable was the supply situation that Lucas ventured to tell Alexander he thought he could support two more divisions in the beachhead. In reply, Lucas received an enigmatic smile. "He is not easy to talk to," Lucas wrote about Alexander, "as he really knows very little of tactics as Americans understand it and I still have trouble because I don't understand the British very well."

Lucas did not know that Alexander and Clark had already decided on the afternoon of February 1 to switch over to the defense. A German counterattack, they believed, was imminent, and on the following day they ordered Lucas to set up strong defensive positions with mines and wire and to hold strong forces in reserve. To give him more strength, they sent him the First Special Service Force, a mixed brigade of 1,800 picked Americans and Canadians. This force arrived at the beachhead on February 2 and went into position along the Mussolini Canal. The next day the 168th Brigade of the 56th British Division arrived to reinforce the 1st British Division. The rest of the 56th British Division—the 167th and 169th Brigades—arrived during the next two weeks.

Ordered to halt all attacks and consolidate his positions, Lucas was regretful. "I hate to stop attacking," he wrote. "We must keep him [the enemy] off balance all we can."

By that time, keeping the enemy off balance was a forlorn hope. The initiative had passed to Kesselring. The VI Corps would soon be fighting for its life.

THE PRELIMINARIES

6 MACKENSEN PLANNED to attack on both sides of the Albano–Anzio road and down that road to the sea. Though he preferred to outflank the Allies instead of hitting them frontally, any enveloping effort west of the road would be exposed to Allied naval guns, a similar endeavor on the east would have to go over ground completely void of cover and crisscrossed by several major canals that would have to be bridged. Only the terrain adjacent to the main road permitted fast movement by tanks. Besides, to get his offensive going before the Allies moved substantial reinforcements into the beachhead, Mackensen needed the shortest possible route into the most vital sector.

The Allied attack started on January 30 disarranged Mackensen's plans. Though the Allies failed to secure the objectives they wanted, they shook up his units, disorganized his offensive preparations, and seized Aprilia (the Factory) that Mackensen regarded as an indispensable springboard for his own attack.

The village of Aprilia, before being leveled by bombs and shells, was a compact cluster of three- and four-story brick buildings designed in 1936 as a model for Fascist farm settlements. The geometrical pattern of the buildings made it look like a factory. Located on a slight rise of ground dominating the countryside, the settlement also had the appearance of a fortress.

Not only did Aprilia offer strong defensive positions. It also controlled the network of roads leading to the south and southeast. The roads now were vital because rain had turned the fields on the Anzio plain into one vast bog.

Before Mackensen launched his decisive attack, he wanted to recapture the Aprilia complex. This required time and forces, and Mackensen had to be economical with both.

While watching Mackensen, Kesselring also had to keep one eye on Vietinghoff and the Tenth Army. When heavy fighting broke out once again at Cassino on February 1, Kesselring informed Mackensen to expect a reduction of his ammunition supplies and possibly even a transfer of some of his units.

In that case, Mackensen responded, he doubted if he would have sufficient strength to eliminate the beachhead. His losses, as a result of the Allied offensive, had already cut sharply into his forces.

Why not, then, Kesselring asked, rush the preparations for his own attack?

Because, Mackensen pointed out, a decisive attack needed careful preparation. The relative weakness of his infantry troops, not only in numbers but also in experience, and short-ages in tanks and artillery gave him, more than likely, but one chance to destroy the beachhead. If the first attempt failed, where would he get additional forces and supplies to try again?

Kesselring had to concur.

Though stability was emerging on the higher echelons of German command at the beachhead, the order of battle on the lower levels remained in large measure an improvisation. Below division level, according to one observer, "the line-up was still a witch's brew." Many units were still arriving. Because Mackensen could seldom afford the time required for units to assemble and reorganize, he had to put units into the line as fast as they arrived and wherever they were needed. The German line was "in a constantly fluid state with an unending succession of arrivals, departures, groupings, regroupings, mergings and partitionings."

Having judged his available forces inadequate for an all-out venture, and having persuaded Kesselring that his view was sound, Mackensen intended first to launch small-scale thrusts to weaken the Allies gradually until he found it possible to launch a larger smash. His first objective was the finger-shaped Allied salient pointing north through the German lines at Campoleone, "positively demanding," as Mackensen's chief of staff saw it, to be counterattacked.

Though Kesselring wanted the offensive to start on February 2, he had to postpone it for three reasons: New indications—in reality Allied deception measures—again led Kesselring to expect new landing operations at Civitavecchia, and he had to alert Mackensen once more to the possible necessity of moving troops there. The Cassino front deteriorated to the point where Kesselring felt compelled to send a battalion of paratroopers from the beachhead to the Tenth Army. And the command post of the I Parachute Corps received a direct hit during an Allied air raid, temporarily knocking out the entire corps communication network.

In spite of all the problems, preparations for attack were completed by February 3. That evening the Germans launched what they considered a small-scale preliminary effort, in no sense the decisive counterattack to push the Allies into the sea.

From a defensive point of view, the Allies had not secured a beachhead of sufficient size. Though Lucas's force had pushed out from the Anzio shore for a distance of 14 miles, the beachhead was dangerously vulnerable to counterattack. There was little room for a defense in depth. A major breakthrough would bring the Germans almost immediately to the sea.

The deepest part of the beachhead terminated in a point sticking out from the rest of the line. This salient, 3 miles long and 1½ mile wide, the British 1st Division held, and as a result, the British front measured approximately 10 miles in length. Fatigued by the offensive exertion at the end of January, reduced in strength by the casualties suffered, the British had little time to prepare for German countermeasures.

In addition to these disadvantages, the Allies were acutely conscious of two others. The beachhead was so small that all of it was within range of German artillery. And the Alban Hills gave the Germans excellent observation posts from which to direct artillery shelling of all parts of the beachhead. As someone said, "The enemy could not only see what he shot at but also shoot at what he saw."

In a maze of deep, brush-covered ravines excellent for concealment, a regiment of the German 65th Division assembled for the attack west of the Albano–Anzio road, while east of the road, screened by a railway embankment, units of the 3rd Panzer Grenadier and 715th Divisions also prepared.

Late in the afternoon of February 3, artillery shells began to fall in some volume on the nose of the British salient. When the fire lifted, a company of German infantrymen assaulted and made a slight penetration. British artillery then spoke up, and by the time darkness fell, the British troops had wiped out the small opening.

This minor effort turned out to be only diversionary, for shortly after midnight, when the Allied troops had settled down confident that they had turned back a German attack of some dimension, German artillery fired again. This time the shells were concentrated on the base of the salient. While infiltrating German infantrymen grabbed the nose of the salient, the main attacking forces launched a two-pronged drive converging on the base. Despite the difficulty experienced by tanks crossing the muddy ground, despite fierce resistance on the part of the British, the German infantrymen striking both sides of the salient cut through the defenses and joined forces on the main road to Anzio. This isolated the British troops in the forward part of the salient.

Holding fast though surrounded, the British fought desperately throughout the day under leaden skies and a drizzling rain that kept Allied planes on the ground. British tenacity finally paid off. After taking heavy losses, the Germans relaxed their pressure. As the German grip weakened, the British broke the hold and expelled the Germans from the Campoleone salient.

Considering the forward units of the 1st British Division still dangerously exposed, Lucas ordered the troops to withdraw to a more defensible line. In close contact with the enemy and still under enemy pressure, the British made a skillful withdrawal during the night of February 4. They lost 2½ miles of ground and somewhat more than 1,400 men (of whom, according to German claims, 900 were taken prisoner). But they re-established a cohesive defensive line.

Though the Germans had eliminated the salient and the threat to Albano and Highway 7, they lost probably 800 men, of whom 300 were prisoners. Most important, they had failed to take Aprilia (the Factory) and the ground Mackensen considered essential for a decisive counterattack.

Mackensen had meanwhile asked Kesselring for another corps headquarters. Kesselring, in compliance, transferred the LXXVI Panzer Corps headquarters from the Adriatic side of the Tenth Army line to the beachhead, and on February 4 this headquarters assumed command of the middle and eastern sectors. The I Parachute Corps headquarters, retaining control of the western portion of the line, received responsibility for building a rear defensive line between the Tiber River and Albano and took tactical command of the Rome area.

While the Germans were making these changes, Lucas was setting up a line of defense behind his front. He instructed the troops to hold the ground they had. But as a last resort, they could fall back to what he called a final beachhead line. Less than 3 miles in the rear of the British front, about 5 miles behind the Americans, the final beachhead line, which Lucas ordered strongly fortified with barbed wire and mines, coincided with the initial beachhead line occupied on the third day of the invasion, January 24. Behind this line, Lucas made clear to his subordinate commanders, there could be no withdrawal. A German penetration of these positions would mean the end. The German "thinks he can drive me back into the ocean," Lucas wrote grimly in his diary that night. "Maybe so, but it will cost him."

Because his flanks were easily defended, Lucas placed one regiment of the 45th U. S. Division on the left along the Moletta River, the Canadian-American First Special Service Force on the right along the Mussolini Canal. In the critical central sector, he reduced the size of the 1st British Division front, giving the British responsibility for the area west of the Anzio–Albano road. He reinforced the British with the 509th Parachute Battalion and part of the 504th Parachute Regiment. The 3rd U. S. Division remained where it was, facing Cisterna.

In corps reserve Lucas held the 1st Armored Division, a sizable force despite the fact that one of its two combat commands was still at Cassino waiting for a breakthrough to be achieved into the Liri valley. Located near the Albano road in an extensive area of tangled undergrowth, scrub trees, and bog known as the Padiglione Woods, the armored troops were also organizing the final defensive line behind the British. Also in corps reserve were two regiments of the 45th Division, backing up the 3rd Division in the Cisterna sector and fortifying the area fronting the west branch of the Mussolini Canal. Both reserve forces were ready to counterattack, on corps order, any penetration of the final beachhead line.

All the work involved in fortifying defensive positions had to be done at night. In addition to placing wire entanglements and mines across the front, the troops constructed a system of mutually supporting strongpoints based on the stone farmhouses. The upper floors of the farm buildings provided excellent positions for snipers and observers. The ground floors, strengthened with sandbags and timber, gave shelter for machine guns and antitank weapons.

Inspecting the beachhead on February 6, General Clark was struck by the reduced strength of the British division. In addition to being short in combat troops, the division had lost many antitank guns in the fighting. The 3rd Division also needed replacements badly, at least 2,400, Clark judged. Though he would make every effort to send replacements to the beachhead in order to keep all forces up to authorized levels, the problem would remain chronic throughout the month.

Approving Lucas's defensive preparations, Clark reminded the corps commander to be ready to go over to the offense when the German pressure slackened. In order to permit Lucas to give his undivided attention to the tactical situation, Clark sent up a small staff of logisticians from his Fifth Army headquarters to take charge of the supply operations in the beachhead.

The front was rather quiet on February 7. Not so in the rear areas.

At ten minutes after eight in the morning, twenty German planes—Focke-Wulf 190's and Messerschmitt 109's—dived out of the sun and attacked Anzio and Nettuno. Bombs landing near the VI Corps command post in Nettuno blew up three ammunition trucks, destroyed several buildings, and killed and wounded a dozen men. Lucas moved his command post underground that day, into a large wine cellar.

About half past eleven, fifteen planes bombed and strafed the harbor area, damaging one LCI and one LCT, killing 30 men and wounding 40.

At a quarter after three, another raid. But this flight was

pursued by Spitfire planes. In an attempt to gain altitude, one German pilot under attack jettisoned his bombs. Several fell on the 95th Evacuation Hospital, killing 28 medical personnel and patients, wounding 64, and damaging X-ray and surgical equipment.

Though successful, the German raiders did not escape unscathed. Allied antiaircraft guns that day destroyed seven planes, damaged approximately twelve. Allied fighter planes claimed to have destroyed another seventeen German aircraft and to have probably destroyed twelve more.

Increased German air attacks against Allied rear areas foreshadowed Mackensen's second attack. Having eliminated the Campoleone salient, he now strove to gain the Factory. His blow started at nine o'clock that evening, February 7, with an artillery preparation. Fifteen minutes later small groups of infiltrating German infantrymen fought across the Moletta River and eastward toward the Albano road, pushing deep into British positions. Though some German troops even reached the main road, these were quickly wiped out.

At ten o'clock that night contingents of the 3rd Panzer Grenadier Division infiltrated the British right flank in small groups. Armed with machine pistols and machine guns, these troops cut British communications and organized small pockets of resistance deep within the British lines. Around midnight units of the 715th Division added their weight and almost reached the Factory.

Despite the fire from three Allied cruisers (two British and one American), the Germans came close to taking the Factory. British reserves committed on the afternoon of the next day, February 8, regained some of the lost ground, thus permitting new positions to be organized. Though the 1st Division was again seriously weakened by casualties, the British had effectively checked Mackensen's assault.

"I wish I had an American Division in there," Lucas wrote that night. "It is probably my fault that I don't understand them better. I think they suffer excessive losses. They are certainly brave men but ours are better trained, in my opinion, and I am sure that our officers are better educated in a military way."

Mackensen resumed his strike against the Factory early on February 9. He used the same pattern—artillery preparation, infantry infiltration, then the main blow—and forced the British back. American paratroopers and tankers entered the fray to give the British time to reorganize and consolidate positions. But Mackensen gained Aprilia. Though eighty-four medium bombers on their way to attack supply dumps around Valmontone were diverted en route and dropped their loads on German troop assembly areas near Campoleone, the Germans hung grimly to the ground Mackensen wanted for his decisive attack.

The fighting slackened late that afternoon. Both sides had taken heavy losses, and both were near exhaustion. Both consolidated their positions and reorganized their forces.

Again, on the morning of February 10, Mackensen attacked in dogged determination, this time for ground to protect the Factory.

"Things get worse and worse," Lucas wrote.

After bitter fighting the 65th Division took what Mackensen wanted, lost it to a British counterattack, retook it in the evening.

This time, after three days of fighting, Mackensen had the Factory well in hand. There he had to pause. Before he could launch his overwhelming attack, he had to have fresh troops.

Drained of energy, reduced to an estimated half of normal strength, the British 1st Division was in no condition even to hold the positions to which it had been forced back. Lucas therefore assigned a good part of the British front to the two regiments of the 45th Division he had been holding in reserve.

To these regiments he gave the task of regaining Aprilia.

Had both regiments attacked, they might have retaken it. Instead, one regiment received the mission. The regiment delegated the job to a battalion. The battalion in turn assigned the task to a rifle company. Supported by another rifle company and by two companies of tanks, the designated assault company attacked, but could do little. When the leading tank in support moved through an underpass and drove boldly toward Aprilia, it fell prey at once to a direct shell hit. The second tank in column managed to go 200 yards farther before being blown up, the victim of a mine. Though a handful of infantrymen fought their way into Aprilia behind a screen of smoke, the troops found themselves opposed by a battalion of Germans emerging from deep cellars, which had protected them from American artillery fire. The Americans were driven out.

Another attempt to recapture Aprilia on the following day also met with defeat. With eight tanks lost in two days and several others damaged, with the assaulting rifle company reduced to three officers and forty men, General Lucas called off the struggle. A major effort, he decided, would be necessary to take back the Factory. And this, he judged, was hardly feasible at the moment.

With this, the fighting diminished. Both sides took a respite.

Lucas could find little comfort in the situation. Nor could he discover any in a directive that arrived from Alexander. General Alexander, the message read, "considers it essential to the achievement of our object which is to drive the enemy North of Rome, the 6 Corps should resume the offensive immediately the tactical situation permits."

To Lucas, the message had little meaning. "This is becoming a war of attrition," he remarked in his diary. "Until I am considerably reinforced I can't do much about it."

Having secured the necessary springboard, Mackensen began immediately to prepare for his decisive thrust down both sides of the Albano–Anzio highway. On the one hand he had to get it off quickly, for there was a real question in his mind as to whether the German forces were strong enough to accomplish their aim. On the other hand, Mackensen was wary of attacking before all preparations were complete, for he doubted whether he would have another chance.

Mackensen's preparations included the regrouping of his units in order to obtain a more homogeneous order of battle. Additional forces which were arriving at the beachhead increased his strength. Though he handed several units of the 71st Division over to the Tenth Army, he received the veteran 29th Panzer Grenadier Division in exchange. The 114th Division completed its move from Yugoslavia, and the 362nd Division in its entirety reached the beachhead from northern Italy. A special demonstration unit, the Berlin-Spandau Lehr Regiment, a crack infantry outfit used to show troops in training how to execute an assault, also arrived; this force came from Germany as Hitler's contribution to spearhead the attack.

In Hitler's mind, considerable political significance rode on the outcome of the battle at Anzio. He believed that if the Germans succeeded in destroying the beachhead, this would prompt the Allies to postpone their invasion of northwest Europe. Thus, speed and daring were essential. After reviewing Mackensen's plan at his East Prussian headquarters, Hitler also made many suggestions. These had to be regarded as instructions whether or not Hitler intended them as such.

One of Hitler's "suggestions" was to attack on a very narrow front.

But massing forces on a narrow front, Mackensen believed, would be bad. Not only would this afford a better target for Allied guns and planes but it also, in Mackensen's opinion, would preclude coming to grips with the main defenses and with the enemy reserves. Attacking on a broader front, Mackensen felt, would pin down greater numbers of enemy forces and increase the power of the thrust at the vital point.

Kesselring agreed with him. But how could they take issue with the Fuehrer?

Hitler also wished to have a creeping barrage "reminiscent of those used in World War I," as he put it. The idea was simply not feasible. The Germans did not have nearly enough ammunition for this kind of wasteful expenditure.

Contrary to suggestions like these, Hitler also issued one specific instruction. He "categorically ordered" the Infantry Lehr Regiment, "which he valued particularly highly," Mackensen later recalled, to be assigned the critical task of making the main effort. Though the troops had never been in combat, they had impressed Hitler with their smartness in training. They were also politically reliable. They would do the job.

Setting D Day for February 16, Mackensen ordered the I Parachute Corps to attack west of the Albano–Anzio road with the 4th Parachute and 65th Divisions in a subsidiary effort; the LXXVI Panzer Corps to make the main effort east of the road in two waves. The first wave, consisting of the Infantry Lehr Regiment, the 3rd Panzer Grenadier, 114th, and 715th Divisions, was to make the breakthrough. The second wave, the 29th Panzer Grenadier and 26th Panzer Divisions, was to exploit the penetration and drive to the coast. Weakening all other sectors as much as he dared, Mackensen ordered continual small-scale assaults to be made along the entire front, particularly by the 4th Parachute and Hermann Goering Divisions, in order to conceal the point of his major blow.

Hitler figured the attack had a good chance to succeed. Mackensen had superior numbers in ground troops and heavy artillery to offset Allied air and naval superiority. By this time, the Fourteenth Army had more than 125,000 troops, as compared with approximately 100,000 under Lucas. In a ringing order of the day to the German forces, Hitler exhorted them to remove the beachhead "abscess" from the Italian coast. He knew they could do it, and he expected them to accomplish it within three days.

Mackensen ordered no unusual assault operations carried

out during the night before the attack, for he hoped to preserve some measure of surprise. He warned tanks and assault guns not to operate ahead of infantry because of strong Allied antitank defenses and extensive mine fields. He instructed tankers to move to their battle stations between midnight and 4 A.M. He also arranged for the *Luftwaffe* to conduct nuisance raids on the Allied front lines.

Despite Mackensen's careful preparations, his army was handicapped, he felt, by certain definite shortcomings. Some units recently arrived from Germany, the Infantry Lehr Regiment in particular, had not had enough time to become oriented. Some units were missing various quantities of their organic vehicles. Not enough artillery ammunition was on hand, he believed, for a large-scale attack. Nor could the Germans count with confidence on consistent air support. And the concentration of large numbers of men in a very narrow attack zone bothered him.

Because of these conditions, Mackensen asked Kesselring to postpone the attack for one or two days.

Kesselring refused. Optimistic, unwilling to listen to what displeased him, Kesselring was sure that the Germans would drive all the way to Anzio, wipe out the beachhead, and return in triumph to Germany to parade through Berlin displaying to cheering multitudes the prisoners of war they had captured.

How different was this from Mackensen's sober view. Like Lucas, Mackensen was fundamentally a technician. He was conservative. He lacked the verve and fire of Kesselring, but he was thorough. Interested in details, he paid close attention to them. The bold and sweeping generalization he found distasteful. He was careful, steady, a worrier.

Unlike in temperament and outlook as well as in tactical judgment, Kesselring and Mackensen had been uncomfortable with each other for some time. Even before Anzio, they both had recognized the long-standing and deep-rooted differences of opinion that separated them.

Since coming to the beachhead, Mackensen had twice asked to be transferred to another command. Kesselring had refused. Mackensen, Kesselring considered, well balanced his own predilections.

Once again, on the eve of the decisive attack, Mackensen tried to tender his resignation. Genuinely doubting the ability of his forces to push the Allies into the sea, he was unable to convince Kesselring that a realistic appraisal of the German chances of success was less sanguine than Kesselring believed. If the commander himself lacked confidence in his projected effort, should he not be relieved?

No! Kesselring said. He would not hear of it. He was a confirmed optimist, and nothing would change him. He dismissed the problems that Mackensen raised, for he was sure that vigor and will and courage would in the end prevail.

Something of this same sort was going on among the commanders on the other side of the front, where hope and despair alternately seized men's minds and hearts, where the difficulties of a coalition endeavor exaggerated sensibilities, where clashes occurred between friends because they were overworked and worried.

When General Alexander visited the beachhead on February 14, his poise and presence struck Lucas as being close to nonchalance, almost patronizing. How, in the midst of a desperate situation, could one be so unaffected, so unconcerned? Alexander irritated him. "Always optimistic," Lucas commented. Alexander had great ideas, but he waved aside as affairs of little moment and less import such vital things as manpower and artillery ammunition.

On the following evening of February 15, General Lucas inscribed some words in his diary that could have been motivated only by an intuitive feeling. Perhaps a stinging of his left ear told him that someone was talking about him in uncomplimentary fashion. Maybe it was telepathy. Whatever it was, his diary entry came remarkably close to the mark.

"I am afraid," Lucas wrote, "the top side is not completely satisfied with my work. . . . They are naturally disappointed that I failed to chase the Hun out of Italy but there was no military reason why I should have been able to do so. In fact," he concluded, "there is no military reason for 'Shingle.' "

He could not have known that Alexander, at almost that precise moment, was sending a message to General Brooke in London to complain about Lucas's leadership of the VI Corps.

He was disappointed, Alexander told Brooke, and disturbed because of the negative quality of command in the beachhead and the absence of the required drive and enthusiasm to get things done. The reason why greater progress had not been made at Anzio was a lack of initiative, an inability to organize an attack on the part of the VI Corps commander. The command, Alexander feared, had become depressed by events. To discuss the problem, Alexander informed Brooke, he had called a meeting for the following day with Wilson, Devers, and Clark. What he wanted to discuss was how to get someone at the beachhead who was "a thruster like George Patton."

To what extent Alexander's dissatisfaction was motivated by factors not bearing directly on Anzio, to what extent his feeling was rooted in events occurring elsewhere is, of course, impossible to say. Still, it was perhaps no mere coincidence that the Cassino front had burst into flame that day, February 15. An armada of heavy bombers executed the controversial bombardment of the Abbey of Monte Cassino. Though Clark had almost violently opposed the bombardment, Alexander had sanctioned the bombing because of pressure from Dominion troops serving under him. The troops from New Zealand and India who were to follow the bombers and assault the formidable Cassino defenses wanted the monastery leveled. And Alexander had had to give in to their wish, for he could not bear to think that his refusal to bomb the monastery would later be referred to as the vital factor that had prevented a breakthrough into the Liri valley, the gateway to Rome.

The abbey had been bombed. But, like the Americans who had tried before them, the New Zealanders and the Indians failed to make much progress at Cassino. If the attack had succeeded in forcing an entrance across the Rapido and into the Liri valley, would Alexander have complained about the VI Corps leadership at Anzio?

In any event, Alexander and Clark conferred on February 16. Without mentioning the message he had sent to Brooke on the previous evening, Alexander told Clark he was disappointed in the way Lucas was handling the corps in the beachhead.

General Clark admitted he, too, was somewhat dissatisfied. But he wondered where Alexander had secured his information about the corps leadership.

Before replying, Alexander elaborated to some extent on why he believed Lucas to be unfit for the command. He was older than his age would indicate, he was physically and mentally tired, he had no flash, he had no familiarity with the details of the changing tactical situation. This information, Alexander finally admitted, came essentially from the commander of the 1st British Division.

Well, Clark said, as long as they were being frank, he might just as well reveal that all three American division commanders, as well as Lucas, had told Clark they had no confidence in the British division commander.

General Alexander was shocked.

He was making no request to relieve the British commander, Clark said, and he agreed that it might be advisable to remove Lucas. But he would insist on one thing. Lucas was to be hurt as little as possible; for he had, in Clark's opinion, performed well. Though he had probably lacked aggressiveness, it was ridiculous to think that he could have gone all the way to the Alban Hills or to Rome. Had he tried that, Clark said, he would have been cut off from the beachhead and would have lost the great bulk of his corps.

Whether Alexander agreed with this line of reasoning, he did not say. But the upshot of the discussion was agreement to appoint two deputy commanders of the corps, one an American to take over eventually the corps command, the other a British officer to help with the British components of the beachhead force.

On the same day, February 16, General Devers was visiting Anzio. He was impressed with the great pride that Lucas took in pointing out the merits of his achievement—Lucas said he could unload forty vessels each day; he had 498 guns and 350 tanks in the beachhead.

Lucas's notes of his conversation with Devers stressed a different subject. Devers had implied, Lucas wrote in his diary, that as soon as Lucas had gotten ashore at Anzio, he should have gone on as fast as possible to disrupt enemy communications. This, Devers had intimated, was what higher headquarters believed. "Had I done so," Lucas wrote, "I would have lost my Corps and nothing would have been accomplished except to raise the prestige and morale of the enemy. Besides," he added, "my orders didn't read that way."

When Devers returned to Clark's headquarters on the following day, February 17, both men agreed on the desirability of relieving Lucas. He was, both felt, extremely tired. They decided to make Lucas Clark's deputy Fifth Army commander while Devers tried to get Lucas an assignment in the States. The most important thing was to keep from hurting him unnecessarily.

On that day Lucas learned of the appointment of the two deputy corps commanders. "I think this means my relief," he wrote. But he hoped desperately against it. "I hope that I am not to be relieved from command. I knew when I came in here that I was jeopardizing my career because I knew the Germans would not fold up because of two divisions landing on their flank. . . . I do not feel that I should have sacrificed my command [by driving on to the Alban Hills]."

But what was past had gone. What was more important at the moment was the struggle for existence brought on by the German counterattack.

THE COUNTERATTACK

7 ON THE MORNING of February 16, around Cisterna, the Hermann Goering Division launched a feint led by two recently arrived companies of a smart and cocky but inexperienced Parachute Demonstration Battalion. Recognizing the feint for what it was, the 3rd Division called for artillery fire which all but annihilated the two assault companies. In trying to explain why they had done so poorly, captured members of the Demonstration Battalion pointed to an exceptionally high rate of dysentery that had swept the ranks just before the attack. The Americans recognized the symptom well. It afflicted many soldiers of all nationalities who were under fire for the first time.

The diversionary attack launched by the 4th Parachute Division against the British had greater success. The paratroopers were not supposed to go anywhere, merely to pin down the British. But they broke through the 56th Division lines and plunged forward for almost 2 miles, bringing profound anxiety to the Allied command. The penetration compelled the division to commit its scanty reserves—one third of the division was still on its way to Anzio—and hard fighting continued until noon.

Neither corps nor army headquarters on the German side

recognized the extent of the paratroopers' penetration. Had the diversionary effort been strengthened, the Germans might well have made a serious breakthrough. Instead, the fighting petered out. By the end of the day the British had restored their lines, though a map of the front showed a dent nearly a mile deep and almost touching General Lucas's final beachhead "no-retreat" line.

The main attack, meanwhile, had opened with heavy artillery fire on both sides of the Albano–Anzio road. As smoke spread across the battlefield, assault waves struck and overran outpost lines of the 45th Division, which now had all three of its regiments together along a 6-mile front in the critical center of the beachhead perimeter.

The major German blow was struck directly down the road, which marked the boundary between the 157th Infantry on the west and the 179th Infantry immediately to the east. Both regiments had to give way, and a German penetration was in the making. Though the seam between regiments was ripped, it did not give way altogether. The battlefield churned as the 45th Division artillery put out an enormous volume of fire. Dogged resistance and the commitment of regimental reserves prevented the Germans from rolling into rear areas. But in the American sector, as in the British, the front had been pushed back a mile, not far from the final beachhead line.

For all the failure of the Germans to make a real penetration, they had provided many an anxious moment. Here is how it was with the 3rd Platoon of Company G, 157th Infantry, commanded by Lieutenant Ralph L. Niffenegger, who had thirty riflemen and an understrength light machine gun section of eight men and two guns.

Around midnight of February 15, when the 2nd Battalion, to which Niffenegger's platoon belonged, relieved British troops west of the Anzio–Albano road, the platoon was assigned a sector on the extreme left flank, along a small ridge in an area known as the Caves, where a maze of vaulted passageways had been tunneled into some small nearby hills. Niffenegger's mission was defensive. He was to hold at all costs.

About the first thing Niffenegger did after setting up his defenses was to send a four-man patrol to make contact with the adjacent British unit on his left. The British were supposed

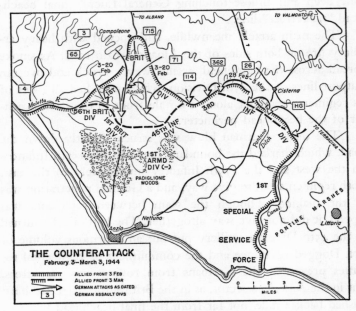

THE COUNTERATTACK
February 3–March 3, 1944

ALLIED FRONT 3 FEB
ALLIED FRONT 3 MAR
GERMAN ATTACKS AS DATED
3 GERMAN ASSAULT DIVS

to be only about 500 yards away, but the patrol could not find them. Niffenegger decided to wait until daylight before sending out another patrol.

A heavy ground fog and haze came with the morning of February 16, reducing visibility to what seemed like arm's length. At six o'clock, in accordance with standing operating procedure in the battalion, though everything was quiet, Niffenegger alerted his platoon for action.

At exactly twenty-eight minutes after the hour, Niffenegger received a routine telephone call from his company commander. The two officers were talking at six-thirty when enemy shells started to fall. The German artillery quickly cut the telephone line, bringing the conversation to an abrupt end.

Niffenegger termed the shelling "probably the heaviest concentration [he] ever endured." When the fire ceased, the platoon stiffened for the infantry attack that was sure to come. Smoke from the exploding shells had thickened the ground haze along the bottom of the ravines, and not much was visible except the tops of some nearby knolls. It was not long before the men saw dim figures there, about 100 yards away. The riflemen and machine gunners opened fire, but the Germans, for they were indeed Germans, moved through the fire apparently unscathed.

Not long afterwards, from a ravine about 75 yards in front of the platoon positions, a group of about forty Germans advanced in a rush. Niffenegger's two machine guns and his riflemen drove the Germans back, dropping about half of them. Some of the wounded crawled back to the ravine. Others lay where they had fallen, moaning. Niffenegger was startled when he realized that the Germans were making no effort to aid their injured comrades.

Checking his foxholes, he found four of his men dead, six wounded. One of the wounded men refused to leave his foxhole for first-aid treatment; he wrapped a bandage around his injured hand and stayed.

During the short lull that ensued, Niffenegger tried to raise his company headquarters by radio. The radio did not carry. He tried the sound-powered phone. The line was dead. A runner volunteered and Niffenegger gave him permission to check the phone line and report to the company headquarters. The runner departed. Niffenegger was never to see him again.

At eight o'clock the haze lifted. To his left about 400 yards away Niffenegger saw British troops withdrawing under heavy fire, men falling as they were hit. Fifteen minutes later Niffenegger became aware of German soldiers moving around his own left flank and rear. Fire from the platoon chased the Germans back into a ravine.

Anxious because of the threat of encirclement, Niffenegger dispatched another runner to the rear with a request for artillery support. The runner managed to get only about 100 yards from the platoon positions before German fire cut him down.

At eight-thirty the Germans attacked again. A few reached the platoon positions on the left, but there the assault lost momentum and stopped. "A few more men and a few more minutes," Niffenegger later recalled, "and the platoon would have been completely overrun."

By this time Niffenegger's situation was critical. One of his two machine guns was out of action with an overheated barrel. Only twenty able-bodied men remained in his command. At least half the ammunition was gone. Nine wounded men who needed medical attention badly could not be evacuated because the routes to the battalion aid station in the Caves were under fire. But worst of all was the fact that the Germans had worked their way around and behind the platoon, completely surrounding Niffenegger's positions.

Niffenegger decided to hold until darkness, then try to withdraw to his company headquarters. But in the early afternoon another German assault group swept up the small rise, overran Niffenegger's 1st and 2nd Squads on the left, and captured eight men. This left the lieutenant with only six men in condition to fight.

Later that afternoon an American combat patrol came up on the rise to see what had happened and to bring Niffenegger a message from his company commander. The platoon was to retire to the Caves at once. Of the original thirty-eight men, eight had been captured, twenty-four killed or wounded.

What Niffenegger had been through was the beginning of what was to be a week-long action called the battle of the

Caves. Because of the deep ravines in this rough country west of the Albano road, it was impossible to develop a continuous line of defense or even to employ artillery effectively against enemy groups that infiltrated between and into the defensive positions. American and British troops fought what was later to be called an epic of defensive warfare at close range. It was a costly engagement, a bloody little war of attrition, in which companies were overrun and entire squads and platoons disappeared without leaving a trace.

Niffenegger's losses on the first day of the German attack were no worse than those sustained by the entire 2nd Battalion, 157th Infantry (45th Division). Of the 43 officers and 936 men on the battalion roster for February 15, only 6 officers and 225 men were still with the battalion a week later; and of these, 90 had returned after having been evacuated for wounds.

The German counterattack on the first day had hardly touched the 180th Infantry, which held the eastern portion of the 45th Division front. Captain Robert A. Guenthner, who commanded Company F in that regiment, did not have it too bad. After a German artillery and mortar barrage struck Guenthner's company at seven-thirty, German infantrymen advanced by short rushes to a point about 400 yards in front of his positions. There the Germans stalled. By ten o'clock the fire on both sides of the line had ceased. Two hours later, after Americans and Germans had both evacuated their wounded, the battle recommenced, this time at long range. The German infantry made no effort to come close. Casualties in Guenthner's company that day totaled 3 killed and 9 wounded.

Despite the fact that they had pushed the British and the 45th Division back about a mile that day, the Germans were disappointed. They had counted on the firepower and shock effect of their tanks to accomplish much more. A frost during the previous night had hardened the ground enough to permit the tanks to move to their battle stations, but the temperature rose in the morning and made the Anzio plain soft and sticky. Tank maneuver in close support of the infantry was impossible. With the tanks confined to the roads, armored operations were insignificant, for the tanks could work only in small groups and only in column. If the lead tank was knocked out, the ones following became immobile and vulnerable to American artillery and antitank fire. As a result of the ineffectiveness of the tanks, the German infantrymen felt deceived. They had expected much more.

Also disappointing was the western debut of a German secret weapon, a miniature tank called the Goliath. No larger than a large dog, the Goliath was loaded with explosives and remotely controlled by electrical impulses transmitted through a long cable attached to the tank. Designed to work ahead of the troops and blow up strongpoints and other obstacles, clear mine fields and barbed wire, and break through concrete walls, the Goliaths failed at Anzio as they had failed in Russia. Regarded by the German engineers who operated them as "a troublesome and rather dangerous toy," thirteen were employed on the first day of attack, and all bogged down. Three were destroyed by Allied artillery. The others were dragged away by the Germans.

Even more disappointing was the performance of the Infantry Lehr Regiment. Made up of excellent human material —Mackensen's remark—the regiment had never faced an enemy in combat. Meeting strong opposition, taking heavy casualties, losing many officers, the regiment suffered a distinct reverse. As the inexperienced troops broke and fled, they robbed the German attack of its momentum.

Kesselring later berated himself for having accepted on hearsay the estimate that the regiment was invincible. He should have known that a home defense unit without fighting experience could not stand up to a major action the first time it was committed. In his considered opinion, Infantry Lehr had performed "disgracefully."

Mackensen's dissatisfaction lay elsewhere. His troops had incurred high losses without having forced the Allies to commit the 1st Armored Division, the considerable force Lucas was holding in reserve. Until the armored division entered the fray, the outcome of the battle could not be decided. But Mackensen had not yet played all his cards. He had not used strong reserves belonging to the first wave of the attack forces. Nor had he thrown the two divisions of the second wave into action.

Kesselring had already suggested committing the two veteran divisions of the second wave. Several times during the day Kesselring had felt that Mackensen should have sent the divisions into the attack. They would have contributed enough weight, he believed, for the Germans to have overrun the Allied line.

Mackensen thought not. In his opinion, the battle was going to last longer than had originally been expected. He had to conserve his forces for the critical moment. Since he hoped to force a breakthrough on the following day, he wished to keep the two divisions in reserve for the final decisive thrust that would destroy the beachhead.

The picture was attractive. Kesselring reluctantly agreed.

That evening, February 16, Mackensen emphasized to his subordinate commanders the importance of allowing the Allies no rest during the night. He wished strong assault parties to continue to attack through the hours of darkness, supported wherever possible by tanks.

The night operations had some success. About half a battalion of the 715th Division worked around both flanks of Company E, 157th Infantry, astride the Albano–Anzio road, the other half struck directly into the company positions. Wiping out the American forward defenses, the Germans forced the defending remnants into a tight perimeter around the command post. Fortunately for the Americans, three tanks of the 191st Tank Battalion were at hand to help the company hold out. By dawn only fourteen riflemen remained. Very little ammunition was left, and all supply routes were cut. Four

German tanks were closing in for the kill when the company commander finally received permission at five o'clock in the morning to withdraw. The Americans fought their way out of the trap, but a dangerous gap was again opened between the 157th and 179th Regiments of the 45th Division. To exploit this hole, the Germans brought up reserves.

At twenty minutes before eight o'clock, about thirty-five planes bombed and strafed the 45th Division. A few minutes later, troops from the 715th, 65th, and 114th Divisions, supported by about sixty tanks, struck into the gap.

The 2nd Battalion, 179th Infantry, took the blow. One rifle company was immediately lost. What remained of the others fell back about a mile to positions barely in front of Lucas's final beachhead line.

At twenty minutes before eleven o'clock, about forty-five planes again bombed and strafed the 45th Division. One bomb struck the command post of the 3rd Battalion, 179th Regiment, and knocked out all communication lines. Exploiting German infantry and tanks again drove into the gap, spread and deepened the penetration. By noon the Germans had driven a wedge 2 miles wide and more than a mile deep into the center of the 45th Division front.

To shorten his line and tie in his flanks, the regimental commander of the 179th Infantry ordered his two forward battalions to pull back 1,000 yards. Made in daylight and in plain view of the Germans, the withdrawal was almost disastrous. Taking heavy casualties, the battalions were torn to shreds. Small groups of men scattered and made their way back to the final beachhead line as best they could. The battalions became little more than company-size units.

With his final beachhead line virtually unmanned in this sector, Lucas put additional resources at the disposal of the 45th Division—more artillery and tanks, four batteries of 90-mm. antiaircraft guns that could fire at ground targets, and the fire of two cruisers offshore. He requested that all available planes be sent to the critical area, a request that was fulfilled that afternoon as all types of Allied bombers flew more than 700 sorties in direct support of the ground forces. General Lucas brought the 1st British Division out of reserve and sent it to take positions backing up the final beachhead line between the 56th and 45th Divisions. He also committed three tank companies, and soon afterwards a tank battalion of the 1st Armored Division for defensive firepower at the threatened spot.

As Lucas expected, Mackensen broadened his attack that afternoon. Committing the reserves of his first assault wave, Mackensen struck into the salient the morning attack had created. As a total of fourteen battalions of infantry and tanks tried to widen the wedge that separated the 157th and 179th Regiments, Mackensen awaited the vital moment of decision, when he would send his exploiting forces to ram home his attack and destroy the beachhead.

The Americans refused to break. The line, though dangerously close to disintegration, remained intact. Supported by a reckless expenditure of artillery, tank, tank destroyer, and mortar fire, the infantry held.

Not everyone was strong. As the pressure began to tell, some men could not withstand the constant grin of death. Captain James H. Cook, Jr., who commanded Company L of the 179th Regiment, saw a tank destroyer crew blow up their vehicle and gun with incendiary shells even though the Germans were nowhere near. The men trickled back to the rear "hysterical and crying."

Despite the inevitable individual breakdowns, despite the German onslaught, when the confusion lifted momentarily at the end of the day, Americans in the sectors of the 157th and 179th Infantry Regiments still occupied Lucas's final beachhead line.

On the 45th Division right, the 180th Infantry remained relatively untouched. Guenthner's Company F had again been attacked, but not intensely. The Germans had concentrated against the 179th on Guenthner's left, and when that regiment gave way, German tanks entered what Guenthner called "this penetrated area." His own left flank was considerably exposed, but the Germans seemed not to notice.

That evening of February 17 Mackensen debated whether he ought to discontinue his attack or commit his second wave of two divisions. Arguing in favor of calling off further effort was the fact that the first wave had incurred serious losses. The fighting strength of each battalion averaged somewhere between 120 and 150 men, about the size of a company. Certainly no one could expect these battered and weary units to make a breakthrough. On the other hand, if the battle was on the verge of being won, "It would be folly," as Mackensen's chief of staff suggested, "to break off now."

Kesselring thought it was probably already too late to win the battle, but he favored continuing nevertheless. Every possible means, he thought, ought to be tried to force a decision. Besides, Hitler would sanction no letup. Appreciating the political as well as the military reasons influencing the Fuehrer, Kesselring ordered the attack to go on.

Mackensen instructed the first-wave forces to attack during the night, while both divisions of the second wave moved up to jump off at four o'clock on the morning of February 18. Instead of exploiting a breakthrough, the two fresh divisions were to try to make the breakthrough themselves. Perhaps they could exploit their own penetration.

What Mackensen had desired to be continued assaults by the reduced and tired elements of the first wave, the Americans saw as night infiltration parties, too weak to do more than harass the front lines. By this time, for example, the German 65th Division had a combat strength of less than a thousand men.

The first thrust at dawn by the fresh units of the second wave was something else. Virtually destroying a battalion of the 179th Infantry before noon, the 29th Panzer Grenadier and 26th Panzer Divisions had made a breakthrough and were ready to push the final few miles to Anzio. But whatever joy the commanders might have had was short-lived. The German units could not continue.

Although the overcast sky prevented Allied aircraft from coming out in force, artillery was heavy and effective. Captain William H. McKay, an observer in a small L-4 cub plane who spotted 2,500 Germans and a column of tanks moving from Campoleone to exploit the opening, radioed the 45th Division Artillery. Within twelve minutes, the corps fire control center had massed the shells of more than two hundred British and American pieces on the target. When the smoke cleared, the German force had disintegrated. Four more times within an hour, McKay broke up German formations by this means.

But what finally stopped the Germans from overrunning the final beachhead line was the courage and determination of the riflemen, machine gunners, and mortarmen who fought at close range and refused to budge.

By noontime, it was obvious that the 179th Infantry, unless immediately resuscitated, would fall apart and vanish. One battalion was seriously under strength, another was at less than half strength and exhausted, and the third was shattered to the point of ineffectiveness. All communication lines between regimental headquarters and the battalions were out. The regimental commander was on the verge of collapse from overwork and lack of sleep. In this situation Lucas sent Colonel Darby, former commander of the virtually extinct Ranger Force, to assume command of the regiment on the final beachhead line.

Darby arrived in the regimental command post at two o'clock that afternoon to take over.

The 3rd Battalion commander, after gathering together his pitifully few troops, had come to the headquarters for instructions. He was there when Darby came in. "Sir," he said in a resigned voice, "I guess you will relieve me for losing my battalion."

Darby gave him a friendly pat on the back. "Cheer up, son," he said. "I just lost three of them, but the war must go on."

The remark was not flippant. Darby cared too deeply for his Rangers to be flippant about losing them. But his words had just the right effect on the fatigued and discouraged people at the regimental headquarters. His confidence, energy, and enthusiasm were invigorating.

"Look at that artillery firing," Darby said, pointing vaguely to the sound of outgoing shells rushing over the command post. "That artillery firing is the most beautiful sight in the world. No one can continue to attack through that."

The men believed him.

Darby's estimate of the regiment's low effectiveness led him to suggest falling back from the final beachhead line. If he could move back to the concealment of the Padiglione Woods, he could better reorganize the exhausted and dispirited command.

No, said the 45th Division commander. The final beachhead line would be held at all costs.

O.K., said Darby, and proceeded to dam up his portion of the defensive line the best he could. Fortunately, for some inexplicable reason, the German attack, having butted furiously against the 179th Infantry without crashing through, now shifted to the right against the relatively untouched 180th Infantry.

Guenthner's Company F of that regiment had still been in place that morning when the German attack had opened. Just before dawn he received what he judged to be the heaviest artillery and mortar barrage the Germans had yet laid down. The shells cut his communication wires about the time he saw German infantrymen creeping forward on his left. Threatened with being outflanked, Guenthner radioed battalion headquarters and requested permission to withdraw 600 yards to alternate positions that had been previously prepared. The battalion commander approved. As Guenthner disengaged his company and retired, artillery covered his withdrawal. Unaware of the pullback, German mortars and artillery pounded Guenthner's former positions for two hours. When the German fire lifted, Guenthner knew he had not long to wait for the enemy assault.

Launching their heaviest attack of the day later that afternoon, the Germans struck the 45th Division once more. For four hours confusion and desperation characterized the fighting. But British infantrymen and American tankers shored up the threatened final beachhead line. And when the noise ceased and the smoke lifted, it was plain for everyone to see—the Germans had failed to achieve their breakthrough.

In Guenthner's area, German infantrymen crept forward again, continuing to exploit Guenthner's open left flank. They were ready by three o'clock to envelop the company once more. Again Guenthner requested permission to withdraw another 900 yards. Again the battalion commander agreed. This time, the Germans did not pursue. Soon after nightfall Guenthner received an order to fall back an additional 1,000 yards. He did so, and this put him squarely on the final beachhead line. But now his left flank was solidly tied in with a firm position held by American armored infantrymen.

For Guenthner that was all there was to it. The apprehension and the strain belonged to the immediate past. Looking *back* on the three days of the German counterattack, he didn't think the battle had been very difficult. Yet the strange thing was the size of the company Guenthner had left. In those three days of action, he had lost two officers and one hundred men, more than half his command.

That evening the Germans concluded that their decisive attack had failed. Small thrusts on the morning of February 19 were nothing more than attempts to consolidate the gains the Germans had made. Counterattacks that afternoon by American tankers and British infantrymen gathered in 400 prisoners and drove the Germans back a mile from the final beachhead line. A final convulsive German effort on the morning of February 20 had little result.

The five-day attack that pushed the Allies to their final beachhead positions had failed to break them and had cost the Germans more than 5,000 men, most of them wounded by shell fragments. Allied artillery, aided by air attacks and naval fire, had been, as one prisoner reported and one interrogator translated, the worst "demorilizive agent." The salient that Mackensen had driven into the 45th Division had become a death trap for his own tanks and infantry.

Promised an easy victory, the German troops were depressed. A serious morale problem arose among the troops opposing the Allied beachhead.

Yet the Allies were in hardly better shape. The ground forces had lost 5,000 men. The 45th Division alone had 400 killed, 2,000 wounded, another 1,000 missing. To these, add 2,500 victims to exposure, exhaustion, and trenchfoot among those who had lived through freezing days in foxholes half filled with slush and water; they are euphemistically called non-battle casualties.

After a month of existence, the Anzio beachhead had produced a tremendous number of losses on both sides. The Allies had sustained a total of almost 19,000 casualties—2,000 killed, 8,500 wounded, 8,500 missing. German losses were probably about the same. Almost 40,000 casualties among forces numbering approximately 200,000 men was a twenty per cent loss. But since by far the greater proportion of the casualties came out of the combat units, the fighting forces at the beachhead were reduced almost to impotence. Unless one or the other of the adversaries could do something quickly, both faced the unpleasant prospect of stalemate.

On February 22, exactly one month to the day after the amphibious landing at Anzio, General Lucas was relieved from command of the VI Corps. The action was taken, they said, not because he had failed to take the Alban Hills but because Alexander thought him defeated, Devers believed him tired, and Clark saw him as worn out. Explaining that he "could no longer resist the pressure . . . from Alexander and Devers," Clark removed Lucas without prejudice. He had not lost confidence in Lucas, Clark told him, for he felt that Lucas had done all that could possibly have been expected of him.

Though shocked by the actual event, Lucas was not entirely surprised. What bothered him most of all—"I thought I was winning something of a victory."

Clark thought so too. Lucas, he felt, could have taken the Alban Hills, but he could never have held them. Had Lucas moved at once to the high ground, he would have so extended his corps that the Germans would have annihilated his forces. That was why Clark had given Lucas an order so carefully phrased—to keep the VI Corps from receiving a "foolhardy mission." He had not thought it wise to tell Lucas beforehand, "Take the Alban Hills." For Lucas would then have been obliged to drive for that objective before securing a strong beachhead.

As Clark looked back on the Anzio operation, he was not disappointed by Lucas's conduct of the battle during the first few days of the landing. As a matter of fact, he approved Lucas's caution. Alexander, he felt, was the one who was dissatisfied. But then British intelligence was "always," in Clark's opinion, "overoptimistic about the German resistance in Italy." The Germans had concentrated forces at Anzio much faster than the British had believed possible. Clark himself had felt that Anzio had little chance of success because the Allied force lacked sufficient strength. One more division might have made the difference, but the lack of shipping, of course, prevented that.

Long after the event, when Clark pondered the fighting at Cassino and at Anzio, he thought it might have been better to have kept his own forces concentrated at Cassino rather than splitting off part of them on what he called a "dangerous and unorganized beachhead," where a powerful German counterattack might well have wrecked the entire Allied campaign in Italy.

Yet it was true that Lucas had been less than aggressive. Lucas had made one serious error, and for this only he was at fault. He had failed to capture Cisterna and Campoleone when taking them would have been easy. A secure hold on these key places, Clark felt, would have given the VI Corps such a firm anchor on its beachhead that the Germans might have decided against attack. In this case—purely speculation, of course—the Germans would have had to fall back from Cassino and, probably, beyond Rome.

Almost everyone else felt much the same way about Lucas's chances of getting to the Alban Hills. In Washington, General Marshall believed that Lucas could have reached the hills, but had acted wisely in refraining from doing so. "For every mile of advance," Marshall later said, "there were seven or more miles [to be] added to the perimeter." And surely Lucas did not have enough men to get to the high ground, to hold it, and to make secure the beachhead and the port.

What Alexander more than anyone else had expected was that the threat posed by Anzio, coupled with the attack on the Cassino front, might force the Germans to withdraw. An advance *toward* the hills was exactly what Alexander thought possible, not a helter-skelter rush *to* the heights. It was for this reason that he fully agreed, when visiting the beachhead in the early days of the operation, with Lucas's decision to safeguard what had been gained and to push cautiously toward the eventual objective.

What inclined Alexander toward relieving Lucas from command was his feeling that Lucas had become unequal to the physical demands of the developments at Anzio. He sensed that Lucas, "harried looking and under tremendous strain, would not be able to stand up physically to the hard, long struggle which by that time it was clear the Anzio operation would involve."

The misfortune at Anzio, from Lucas's viewpoint, was that by the time Lucas was ready to make his major effort to threaten the German lines of communication, the Germans had brought together sufficient forces to block him. But even more unfortunate was the fact that Allied intelligence had overestimated the actual German strength and thus fed the virus of hesitation. These intelligence estimates became a myth that explained something that became inevitable simply because it had happened that way. The Germans had stopped Lucas's attack, and they had done so because, so the story went, they were, by then, stronger.

Lucas's opportunity to do something else had come and gone, and after the first few days he no longer had a choice. And that was how Lucas finally saw it.

The only thing that ever really disturbed me at Anzio, except, of course, my inability to make speedier headway against the weight opposing me, was the necessity to safeguard the port. At any cost this must be preserved as, without it, the swift destruction of the Corps was inevitable. . . . My orders were, to me, very clear and did not include any rash, piece-meal effort. These orders were never changed although the Army and the Army Group Commanders were constantly on the ground and could have changed them had they seen fit to do so.

Despite his belief that he could not have done otherwise, alternative courses of action he might have followed disturbed him. He might have sent a small force, he later admitted, to make a sudden raid inland on the Alban Hills. Had he done so on D Day, the force would certainly have reached the heights. But the troops could not have remained. Why court disaster?

"As it turned out," Lucas wrote, "the proper decision was made and we were able to reach and establish ourselves in positions from which the enemy was unable to drive us in spite of his great advantage in strength."

Yet in his own mind Lucas could not dissociate his being relieved of command from the cautious decision he had made upon landing. They said he was tired, worn out, too old. But they were disappointed because he had not fashioned a threat large enough to prompt the Germans to withdraw from Cassino.

That was why, Lucas kept repeating, the whole idea of the Anzio operation was a mistake. Lacking enough forces for a bold push from the beachhead, Lucas had never expected to advance to the Alban Hills. His main mission, according to his interpretation, was to take the port and sufficient ground to protect it.

Part of Lucas's preoccupation with the port of Anzio no doubt came from naval advice. "No reliance," naval planners had made perfectly clear, "can be placed on maintenance over beaches, owing to the probability of unfavorable weather." A port in working order was absolutely essential, then, if supplies were to get to the beachhead forces.

As for the idea of taking Rome, Clark had told Lucas frankly, "You can forget this goddam Rome business."

But could Lucas have gotten away with the gamble of an immediate drive to the Alban Hills? Should he have exploited the complete surprise he found he had gained upon landing at Anzio? Might he possibly have cut the German lines of communication? Would quick success have led to an immediate surge into and beyond Rome?

According to Westphal, Kesselring's chief of staff: "The road to Rome was open, and an audacious flying column could have penetrated to the city. . . . The enemy remained astonishingly passive."

Suppose Lucas had made an immediate aggressive move to

the heights dominating the southern approaches to Rome. Could the Germans have withstood a dynamic thrust as successfully as they countered a static front? Would the Germans have dared to hold opposite both Anzio and Cassino if an Allied force was ensconced on the Alban Hills?

No one would ever know. But many commanders, including Lucas himself, and particularly Alexander, could not shrug off the wisp of a nagging thought. A bluff prosecuted with imagination and daring, carried through with vigor might have worked. A "thruster like George Patton," as Alexander had said, might have done it.

And for not having tried, Lucas could not altogether, nor would he ever, be forgiven.

THE AFTERMATH

8 Lucas DEPARTED from the beachhead a broken man. After serving nominally as Clark's deputy for three weeks, he left Italy for England, where he called on Eisenhower.

He talked about Anzio of course. He did not criticize his superiors, Alexander and Clark, or their conduct of the battle. But he told Eisenhower he had frequently been in a quandary regarding their intentions. He felt that he had been relieved from command at Alexander's insistence. He pictured himself as "simply a soldier" who had carried out orders with which he was not in sympathy.

What struck Eisenhower most about Lucas was his attitude of defeat—Lucas could not get out of his mind the optimism of the German prisoners taken at the beachhead, their certainty that Germany was going to win the war.

Returning to the United States, Lucas became commander of the Fourth Army. To go from corps to army command was a promotion.

Among the able candidates at the beachhead who could have replaced Lucas were three British officers, each of whom would have made an excellent corps commander—Major General V. Evelegh, who had been deputy corps commander, a very fine fellow, according to Lucas, and a great help in directing the activities of the British troops; Major General W. R. C. Penney, the 1st Division commander; and Major General G. W. R. Templer, who commanded the 56th Division.

But the preponderance of strength in the beachhead was American, the VI Corps headquarters was American, and it would be an American who would take Lucas's place.

Three division commanders were well qualified. Major General William W. Eagles, a "quiet, determined soldier, with broad experience," according to Lucas, had served as deputy commander of the 3rd Division through the invasions and campaigns of North Africa and Sicily before replacing in Italy four months earlier the ailing commander of the 45th Division. In command of the 45th since then, Eagles, in Lucas's opinion, had become "one of our most accomplished division commanders." He would be an excellent choice to take over the corps. Yet he was the junior division commander in the beachhead.

An aggressive fighter and combat leader, Major General Ernest N. Harmon had commanded the 2nd Armored Division in the North African campaign before taking command of the 1st Armored. He was the senior American commander at the beachhead, but he was also the least tactful. A big, bluff, energetic man with a barrel chest and a gravel voice, he had a genius for saying the wrong thing, for rubbing people the wrong way. Though his obvious competence and the record of his past performance justified a promotion to corps command, he could hardly be a good choice for a sensitive position in a coalition venture.

The selection thus quite naturally devolved upon Major General Lucian K. Truscott, Jr., who had led the 3rd Division in the North African, Sicilian, and Italian campaigns. To many observers, there was no question—Truscott was the best division commander in the Mediterranean; he had made his division the best outfit in Italy. Lucas, who judged Truscott "a highly capable officer and a loyal soldier towards both his superiors and his subordinates," had nothing but "the greatest

regard" for him. Truscott had balance and judgment, and he
inspired confidence. At Salerno, at the height of crisis, when
Truscott came ashore and told a division commander on the
beach that the 3rd Division was on its way from Sicily to help,
that commander relaxed, for with Truscott present he felt the
battle as good as won. Reserved in his manner, Truscott was
almost taciturn. But not much escaped his notice, and not much
was beyond the range of his fine intelligence. Solid and fair,
Truscott was much admired by Alexander and the British.

When Clark appointed Truscott as Lucas's deputy and
told him he would eventually get the corps, Truscott's assistant
commander, Brigadier General John W. O'Daniel took over
the 3rd Division. Tough, uncompromising, and aggressive,
"Iron Mike" O'Daniel became universally respected.

With Truscott in command of the beachhead, a subtle
change stole over the Anzio plain, an intangible feeling of hope
took hold of the Allied troops. Unlike Lucas, who had not
often ventured out of his vaulted wine-cellar headquarters and
who even on his infrequent visits to the troops had failed to
project an image of confidence and optimism, Truscott produced the required emotional response. His erect figure and
vigorous movements left no doubt in the minds of those who
saw him—and many did—that the worst was over. The situation would now inevitably improve.

Yet there was no time to settle back. The Germans had
relaxed their pressure on the beachhead perimeter, but this was
merely temporary. Indications were plentiful that the Germans
would soon strike again.

For the Germans, the failure of their offensive down the
Albano road argued for another approach to the problem of
Anzio. But the great political significance and propaganda value
that Hitler attached to the elimination of the beachhead made a
different solution impossible. The only alternative open to
Kesselring and Mackensen was nothing more than where to
choose to make another try.

The only other place where a counterattack could give

any promise of decision was Cisterna, where the lines had remained unchanged during the five-day battle just concluded.
On February 22 Mackensen made this recommendation to
Kesselring. On a considerably wider front than the last attack,
he proposed a thrust from Cisterna to Nettuno. Employing
the Hermann Goering, 26th Panzer, and 362nd Divisions in the
initial push, he would hold the 29th Panzer Grenadiers in reserve, ready to mop up should the assault break through the
Allied defenses. Though he wished to start quickly in order to
gain surprise, he needed to regroup his forces and to stock
sufficient ammunition supplies, and this would require several
days.

With Kesselring's approval, Mackensen set his time of
attack for daylight, February 28. Hoping to deceive the Allies
on the point of his operation, he told the I Parachute Corps to
simulate attack preparations on the western portion of the
beachhead by making widespread raids during the preceding
night, by placing dummy tanks in the area, and by making con-
spicuous vehicle movements.

A day before the scheduled attack, Mackensen requested
Kesselring for a postponement of one day, until the 29th.
Mackensen reported the poor condition of his troops, stressed
their lack of training and battle experience, emphasized the
heavy losses they had taken. But the main reason for postponement was bad weather, which had prevented him from getting
large numbers of tanks and self-propelled guns off the roads
and up close to the line of departure.

Kesselring agreed. For once he was not altogether optimistic. He expected a result not much different from the earlier
efforts. But he had to acknowledge the continuing validity of
Hitler's desire, and he hoped for at least partial success. If he
could compress and reduce the size of the beachhead to a very
small area, he might make the Allies wonder whether they
could hold the beachhead at all. In that case, they might abandon a piece of ground that had become too small to defend.

He therefore approved Mackensen's plan to try to dislodge

the Allies by striking from the opposite corner of the beachhead. He discussed with Mackensen the lessons the earlier attacks seemed to offer and endeavored to remedy the previous mistakes.

The day before the offensive, on February 28, Kesselring visited the troops in a torrential downpour of rain. He had already made up his mind to postpone the jump-off once more. But the units were so full of confidence—stirred, no doubt, by the field marshal's inspiring presence, though Kesselring seemed unaware of this—that he deferred to their wishes. The bad weather would actually favor the Germans by giving them the possibility of attaining local surprise. It would also deny the Allies the benefits of tank support and would hamper Allied planes and naval gunners. Somewhat hopefully, cautiously optimistic, Kesselring allowed the attack to proceed.

On the Allied side, patrols probed the front to determine what the Germans were up to. One of these, from the 2nd Battalion, 504th Parachute Infantry, a combat patrol of thirty men under Lieutenant Navas, set out on February 27 to investigate what the Germans were doing in a cluster of four houses about a mile ahead of the front. The job of the patrol was to move to the houses during the night, send back prisoners, and remain in the area if possible throughout the following day to observe enemy movements.

With little intelligence of German strength and dispositions in the area, with no map of the front or of enemy mine fields, Navas moved out his patrol at nine o'clock on the dark evening of February 27. The front was quiet, and Navas was reasonably certain that the Germans had not detected his departure.

Nearing the four stone houses, the patrol came to a small wood. Before entering the brush, Navas divided his command into two parties, retaining control of one party himself and placing the other under Sergeant Rodjenski.

Hardly had the men entered the scrub forest when some-one set off a trip flare. The patrol froze. In the silent night they heard the sound of hurried movement in the houses ahead. Within a matter of seconds, the motor of a tank or self-pro-pelled gun turned over and caught. Pulling out from behind one of the houses, the vehicle began to throw shells into the woods.

Navas instinctively started to lead a rush toward the house, but he ran almost immediately into a mine field. An explosion underfoot brought him down seriously wounded. As the men of his group followed him, they too ran into mines, and several were wounded. Immobilized, all the men of the patrol hugged the ground.

All except Sergeant Frank Salkowski. Slipping a grenade launcher over the muzzle of his rifle, he got off a few shots. They were good shots or else lucky ones, for the enemy vehicle withdrew behind the house.

Rodjenski was on his feet at once, leading the patrol in a rush on the nearest building. Rifle and mortar fire began to fall in good volume. Obviously, there were too many Germans for the paratroopers to take. Rodjenski ordered them back.

The patrol returned without further incident. Upon reach-ing the line, Rodjenski counted noses. Eight men had been wounded. Lieutenant Navas and three men were missing. Tak-ing seven paratroopers, including Salkowski, Rodjenski went back to the woods. He found all four of the wounded and brought them back. That made twelve casualties in all.

Though unable to accomplish their mission, the men had nevertheless demonstrated the presence of a strong German force, including at least one tank or self-propelled assault gun in the cluster of houses.

This information alone might have been meaningless. But many patrols roamed through the no-man's land between the lines every night. All the insignificant data collected and re-ported, fragmentary though they were, when put together by intelligence officers added up to a picture. The mosaic fashioned from the jigsaw bits and pieces brought back by patrols was never entirely complete, even when supplemented by the observations of artillery spotters, air force pilots, secret agents, and others. Yet the totality of the intelligence estimate provided commanders with a fair idea of the ever-changing composition of the enemy front. It gave them a basis for guessing what the Germans might do.

Like the Allies, the Germans of course carried on their own intelligence activities. The result was a war within a war, a nerve-wracking, endless battle between small groups of men engaged in the dangerous business of reconnaissance, ambush, foray, and raid—all for the purpose of gaining information about the enemy and occasionally for the sake of deceiving him.

During the afternoon of February 28 a German smoke screen along the 3rd Division front concealed last-minute troop movements. Around midnight, German artillery fire that had been striking the British sector shifted to the Cisterna area.

The 3rd Division, though exhausted and reduced in size by six weeks of fighting, had had time to prepare for the German attack. The troops had developed a forward line of defense into a formidable and well-integrated barrier of strong points.

Suspecting what was afoot, the 3rd Division called for and received a tremendous curtain of artillery fire that began shortly before dawn on the morning of February 29 and continued for an hour, plastering the logical avenues of approach for the German assault troops.

Despite the heavy weight of the shelling, it failed to disrupt the German attack. At daylight the Germans struck. Infantrymen and panzer grenadiers immediately overran a company of the 509th Parachute Battalion, situated on the 3rd Division's left.

Only one officer and twenty-two men of the American parachute company survived, and they managed to make their way 700 yards to the rear to the battalion's main line of resistance. There, a back-up company of ninety-six men, supported by plentiful mortars and artillery, stopped the German thrust.

This was the most appreciable success the Germans had. When the 362nd Division, bolstered by tanks of the 26th Panzer and Hermann Goering Divisions, struck the 3rd Division head-on, the impact dented the American forward defensive positions. But that was all.

To the east the 715th Division and two battalions of the 16th SS Panzer Grenadier Division drove against the 504th Parachute Infantry Regiment and made a minor penetration that was soon contained. Hitting against the First Special Service Force along the Mussolini Canal, a task force made up of men from the 715th and Hermann Goering Divisions made no progress.

Heavy clouds and frequent rain squalls prevented Allied planes from flying during the morning, but in the afternoon 247 fighter-bombers and 24 light bombers attacked German tanks and infantry. Though the 3rd Division took heavy losses in hot fighting, a counterattack at the end of the day regained for the Americans the few hundred yards they had earlier relinquished.

Despite high casualties in men and tanks, the Germans continued their attack on March 1, but the result was the same. That evening Truscott congratulated O'Daniel for the defensive stand his men had made—Truscott was "delighted with the way you have stopped the Boche."

At about the same time Kesselring was telling Mackensen to bring his offensive to a halt. Bad weather, the poor condition of the assault troops, inadequate training of the new units, the youth and inexperience of replacements, and the general depletion and exhaustion of the combat troops after the previous weeks of fighting—all had taken their toll. Mackensen was to restrict his offensive operations to local counterattacks.

Clear weather on March 2 that permitted planes to come

out in earnest effectively punctuated the end of the German drive, dispelling any illusions that further effort was practical. On that day 241 B-24 Liberators and 100 B-17 Fortresses, escorted by 113 P-38 Lightnings and 63 P-47 Thunderbolts, dropped heavy loads of bombs immediately behind the German lines. This was an impressive display of heavy bomber might; along with it went strikes by medium, light, and fighter bombers against German tanks, gun positions, and assembly areas.

No one on the Allied side knew it at the time, but the days of major German assaults against the beachhead were at an end. In this last major stroke, the Germans had sustained more than 3,000 casualities and lost at least thirty tanks.

From one Allied point of view, hurried preparations, confusion of orders, faulty communications, and insufficient tank and heavy weapons support had caused the German attack to break down. The slight gains made were "hardly worth an outlay which had included [loss of] 500 prisoners of war."

From another Allied viewpoint, German "efforts to win a victory which would bolster flagging morale at home and restore the reputation of the German Army abroad . . . had brought . . . only a further depletion of already strained resources in equipment and manpower."

To Mackensen, Allied superiority in matériel and the contrasting lack of manpower and matériel on the German side made it clear that the Germans could no longer afford to mount large-scale offensives at Anzio. Because the Germans had to expect the Allies to make simultaneous attacks to get out of the Anzio beachhead and to crack the Cassino line, Mackensen recommended conserving the German fighting strength for defense against the forthcoming offensive. With Kesselring in agreement, Mackensen ordered his divisions to train specially organized and equipped assault companies to carry out small-scale attacks and raids, while mobile units were withdrawn to form reserves.

As Kesselring viewed the situation early in March, he concluded that a lull of some duration would probably occur. Both sides had taken heavy casualties during the fighting in Italy—a good part of the troops engaged having fought since the invasion of Sicily in July, all of them having fought since the beginning of the Italian campaign in September. During this time of waiting Kesselring saw his major task as the need to assemble heavy reserves to withstand a coming shock. For the Allies would be sure to try again to link up the forces still fighting at Cassino with those of the beachhead. Unaware of how few facilities the Allies had for amphibious operations, Kesselring half expected that they might possibly attempt to avoid strenuous overland battle and force a decision more cheaply by making another landing either near Civitavecchia or farther north at Leghorn.

Kesselring therefore sent his chief of staff, Westphal, to Hitler to explain how limited his own possibilities were. He asked Westphal to make two points: First, in the face of a perfectly co-ordinated landing of superior land, sea, and air forces, the Germans could not check an invasion even from well-constructed coastal positions. Second, because German counterattacks as a rule were beaten off by heavy artillery fire and air strikes, the Germans needed special weather conditions or especially favorable terrain in order to register a victory.

The conclusion to be drawn from these points was this: Since the fighting at Anzio had clearly ended in a draw, and since the political and strategic problems of the Italian campaign remained unchanged, the Germans could, in Kesselring's opinion, do nothing more than husband their strength and build up their resources in order to be ready to smash the Allied blow they had to expect in the spring.

Early in March, Westphal went to the Fuehrer's headquarters, where he spent a few days. He spoke with Hitler several times, and in a final interview on March 6 lasting an hour and a half, he at last convinced Hitler that another major attack at Anzio was out of the question for the time being.

On the following day, March 7, Westphal telephoned Kesselring and excitedly informed him it was all right to shelve offensive planning. He returned to Rome on March 8, "elated," as someone recorded, "with the praise received [from Hitler] and the understandings reached."

Kesselring had counted on Hitler's understanding. Several days earlier he had ordered a new defensive line constructed across the Italian peninsula. This line was to start on the west coast near the mouth of the Tiber, tie in with Cisterna (to guard Highway 7), go through Valmontone (to protect Highway 6), continue through Avezzano (to protect the lateral highway leading to Rome's back door), and end at Pescara on the east coast. Called the "C," or Caesar, position, the line was to be ready for defense no later than April 20.

The reason for building this line came from Kesselring's consciousness of the danger threatening Vietinghoff's Tenth Army. Should the beachhead forces somehow break out and cut Highways 7 and 6, they obviously would force the flank of the Tenth Army fighting at Cassino to collapse. Should the balance that had been reached in Italy be upset, Kesselring would try to have the Tenth and Fourteenth Armies fight side by side along the Caesar line to delay, possibly stave off, the fall of Rome.

Doubting whether Hitler, after the losses at Stalingrad and in Tunisia, could afford to lose two more armies, Kesselring tried to guarantee the continued existence of the Tenth and Fourteenth Armies. Even though the Allies might take Rome, he would endeavor to preserve the integrity of his forces and to retard an Allied advance. Somewhere in northern Italy, Kesselring could halt the Allies again. Despite the loss of Rome, he could, Kesselring promised, continue to make possible the prosecution of the war for another year, into 1945.

In England, Prime Minister Churchill had been watching the developments at Anzio closely from the start. When Alexander sent him a message soon after the landing, saying he had "stressed the importance of strong-hitting mobile patrols being boldly pushed out," the Prime Minister quickly replied. "Am very glad you are pegging out claims rather than digging in beachheads," he said.

A week later, when Mr. Churchill wired Alexander, "It would be unpleasant if your troops were sealed off there and the main army could not advance up from the south," he did not realize how prophetic he was. Yet only a few days later, Admiral Cunningham informed him, "The situation as it now stands bears little relation to the lightning thrust by two or three divisions envisaged at Marrakesh."

When Wilson, the theater commander, advised him early in February that "the perimeter was sealed off and our forces therein are not capable of advancing," Churchill was most unhappy.

He was unhappy also because the U. S. Chiefs of Staff were expressing, in a message to him, "some concern" over the progress of operations in Italy. The American chiefs wondered whether the situation was developing into a battle of attrition that could have no outcome save steadily mounting losses without decisive gains. They asked why no large-scale and aggressive offensive had been launched at Cassino. They would be glad, they said, to have some advice on Wilson's future plans.

Churchill passed the message along to Wilson.

Wilson's reply was hardly encouraging. Wilson explained that there had been "no lack of urging from above" to push the offensive at Anzio. Unfortunately, the corps commander had suffered from a "Salerno complex." Having judged his first task as the need to repel the inevitable enemy counterattack, he had allowed himself to be contained. As for the difficulties of getting across the Rapido and past Cassino into the Liri valley, they were far more complex than had been imagined.

Mr. Churchill passed along Wilson's explanation to the

Americans, adding, "All this has been a disappointment to me." Yet he reminded General Marshall and the Americans of the great advantage the Allies were gaining by forcing the Germans to "come in strength and fight in South Italy, thus being drawn far from other battlefields." Even a battle of attrition, he thought, was "better than standing by and watching the Russians fight." And finally, looking for the silver lining, Churchill said the Allies would find many lessons at Anzio useful for the forthcoming cross-Channel invasion.

This apparently satisfied the Americans, but Churchill himself remained upset. A few days later, he asked Wilson how many vehicles had been brought to Anzio. Wilson replied that 18,000 trucks were in the beachhead. "We must have a great superiority of chauffeurs," Churchill noted caustically.

Having hoped "we were hurling a wildcat onto the shore," but having gotten nothing more than "a stranded whale," Churchill gave Alexander some advice on February 10. "I have a feeling," he wrote, "that you may have hesitated to assert your authority because you were dealing so largely with Americans. . . . You are however quite entitled to give them orders."

Alexander made known his discomfiture. After he stopped the German counterattacks, he promised, he would resume the attack inland to get astride the German communications between Rome and Cassino.

When the Germans launched their major counterattack in mid-February, Churchill understood the fury of the fighting. "All hung in the balance," he wrote later. "I had no illusions about the issue. It was life or death. But fortune, hitherto baffling, rewarded the desperate valour of the British and American armies."

Explaining the battle in the House of Commons on February 22, he noted that "a large secondary front in Italy is not unwelcome to the Allies. We must fight the Germans somewhere." Referring obliquely to OVERLORD, he said, "This

wearing battle in Italy occupies troops who could not be employed in other greater operations, and it is an effective prelude to them."

When Jan Christian Smuts, the South African statesman,
wrote to ask whether his understanding was correct—"An isolated pocket has now been created . . . which is itself besieged
instead of giving relief to the pressure against us in the south"
—Churchill gave him a long explanation:

In all his talks with me, Alexander envisaged that the essence
of the battle was the seizure of the Alban Hills with the utmost
speed, and to this end I was able to obtain from the United States
their 504th Parachute Regiment, although at the time it was under
orders to return for "Overlord." . . . the whole operation became stagnant. Needless to say, the logistic calculations all turned
out to be on the overgenerous side and there were very large
margins in hand. No one can deny that this was lucky.

Though he was disappointed, Churchill confessed to Smuts,
he did not regret the operation. For it was vital for the cross-
Channel attack to keep away and hold elsewhere as many Germans as possible. Hard fighting in Italy throughout the spring,
he believed, would give the invasion of northwest Europe "a
perfect prelude and accompaniment."

Early in March Churchill recognized that "Kesselring accepted his failure. He had frustrated the Anzio expedition. He
could not destroy it."

Yet there was now no hope of breaking the stalemate at
Anzio. Nor was there any prospect of an early link-up of the
two separate forces unless the Allies could break the Cassino
defenses. Thus, until the Germans gave way at Cassino, the
beachhead had to be made really secure. The troops had to be
reinforced and supplies had to be stocked not only to withstand siege but to "nourish a subsequent sortie." Building up
the beachhead had to be done quickly, for time was short.
Many landing craft had to depart from the Mediterranean for

participation in OVERLORD. Though the move of these boats had long been postponed, no further delay was possible.

By mid-March, Churchill felt no further anxiety over Anzio, despite his continuing disappointment over the Italian campaign. He had hoped that the Allies would have driven the Germans north of Rome to set free a substantial part of their forces for a landing on the Riviera in support of the invasion of northwest France. But at least they had contained the Germans and held substantial numbers of them pinned down in the Italian peninsula.

In a letter written from England to Washington around the end of February, General Eisenhower gave General Marshall his explanation of what he thought had happened at Anzio. The landing force, he said, was immobile and therefore "could not carry out the promise that was implicit in the situation then existing." What saved the day was the complete Allied command of the sea, which permitted the Allies to support and reinforce the beachhead. "I am convinced it will turn out all right in the end," Eisenhower wrote, "but there will be *no* great destruction of German divisions as a result thereof."

As General Wilson saw it, the beachhead had to be made safe. It had to be organized to hold out for a considerable period of time. There could be no hope of an immediate victory. But the situation at Anzio, he thought, should not be allowed to influence the entire campaign to the point of compelling the Allies to rush preparations for breaking the Cassino front. The Allies had to go slowly and deliberately. "We cannot afford a failure," he informed the British Chiefs of Staff.

With this in mind, Wilson requested additional resources for Italy—more troops, more vehicles, more ships. He had not only to carry out actual operations but also to give the Germans the impression that he was capable of conducting larger operations than were in fact possible. Two new American divisions were coming into Italy, and a third was promised.

More French troops were arriving in Italy from North Africa. And British Commonwealth units were coming from the Middle East. These would give Wilson the additional strength he sought in Italy.

According to Alexander's view, as long as the Anzio beachhead existed, it represented a potential threat to the line of supplies for the Germans at Cassino. If the Germans continued their attacks on the beachhead, they would place a steady drain on their forces that would make them too weak in the end to withstand a hard blow. Thus it was logical for them, in his opinion, to discontinue their attacks in favor of building a strong defensive system, particularly since a comparatively short Allied advance from the beachhead would imperil all the troops on the Cassino front.

To the Allies, Alexander continued, the beachhead was a defensive liability, for it imposed a great drain on naval and air resources. It required, for example, the use of nearly all the LSTs and LCTs available in the theater. But from a tactical point of view, the beachhead offered a base for offensive action in probably the most favorable terrain in Italy, certainly better than anywhere along the Cassino line. Furthermore, an attack from the beachhead would strike against the most vital point in the German defensive system, their lines of communication.

If, therefore, the beachhead could be made secure, if supplies could be stocked there for an attack by three or four divisions striking toward Valmontone, and if this operation could be combined with a deep penetration and rapid advance from Cassino into the Liri valley, there would be a reasonable chance of cutting off and destroying a large proportion of the German forces opposing the Fifth Army.

But before the beachhead could be considered secure, the Allies had to drive the Germans out of Cisterna and Campoleone and transform both areas into a firm base for further advances as well as into strong defensive pivots. Before an advance up the Liri was possible, the Allies had to clear the high ground at Cassino and establish a bridgehead across the Rapido large enough to accommodate superior forces for the drive up the valley.

Thus, the great question remained—how to get enough forces to accomplish the minimum objectives at Anzio while at the same time cracking the Cassino defense.

As though this were not enough, still another requirement had to be met. At least two divisions, probably more, would be needed for the invasion of southern France. Since these forces had to come out of the Mediterranean resources, preparing for this invasion would begin to affect the battle in Italy toward the end of March. The Allies, therefore, had to join the Cassino and Anzio fronts during April at the latest in order to make possible an invasion of southern France at the same time as OVERLORD.

Unless, of course, the southern France landings were canceled.

But, early in March, long-range planning and preparations for invading southern France were continuing. A commander for the operation was selected, and the assumption remained that southern France would be invaded to complement OVER-LORD.

The Americans favored launching the southern France invasion even if it meant depriving the forces in Italy of sufficient strength to capture Rome. But Wilson and the British chiefs strongly opposed withdrawing troops from Italy until Rome was captured.

At the end of March the British chiefs telegraphed the American chiefs to recommend canceling the southern France invasion because it was impossible to withdraw troops from Italy or landing craft from the Anzio beachhead. In view of the fact that it was manifestly impossible to cut the throats of those who were defending at Anzio, the Americans reluctantly agreed. First priority would go to the Italian campaign until the capture of Rome. An invasion of southern France would be launched if the situation in Italy improved. But in any case, landings in southern France could no longer be executed to coincide with the cross-Channel attack. The Anzio operation had killed that.

Yet the argument between the Allied partners was not ended. It would continue.

At the beachhead Kesselring and Mackensen drew tentative plans for an offensive to start at the end of March, either down the Albano road or from Cisterna. But in the end, after once postponing the attack, they decided early in April to abandon the idea. Kesselring was reluctant to commit his two best divisions, the 29th Panzer Grenadier and 26th Panzer; and without them, Mackensen could not see how a large-scale attack could succeed.

The Allies also planned offensive operations. Preliminary plans for a large-scale attack near the Albano road were completed, but there was no serious intent to put the plan into effect, and the idea died.

What Germans and Allies both awaited was the renewal of the offensive in the south. For a week in mid-March the Cassino front flared as the Allies set off a large-scale thrust behind a strike by 500 medium and heavy bombers that dropped 1,200 tons of bombs on Cassino and leveled the town. New Zealanders and Indians, aided by British troops, again fought as hard as men have ever fought anywhere, but again they failed to crack the defenses and open the door into the Liri valley.

When Alexander called a halt to the attack on March 23, the fighting in the Italian peninsula died down. Combat became a series of unco-ordinated small-unit actions, raids, ambushes, patrols, and forays, an occasional sharp skirmish, local in scale, minor in importance. Artillery would fire, men would still be killed and wounded. But for a while at least there would be no full-bodied effort. The opponents had reached a stalemate.

It was easy enough for a visitor arriving at the Anzio beachhead on a beautiful spring day in 1944 to gain the erroneous impression that Anzio was a safe spot. Despite the evidences of destruction around the tiny harbor, there was a cheerful, in-souciant attitude among the inhabitants. Except for a handful of civilians—750 to be exact, all Italian laborers—the popula-tion was entirely in uniform. Twenty-two thousand men, women, and children had been evacuated to Naples soon after the landings, and more than 100,000 troops had taken their places. In apparent unconcern over the danger that struck periodically, the men unloaded ships, trucked supplies to inland dumps, and performed all the myriad duties that comprise the bustle of a military camp. The occasional white plume of water that rose as an enemy shell plunged into the bay had an impersonal air. Yet the next shell to whistle over the beachhead might land in the hold of a ship or blow to pieces a jeep driv-ing through the streets of Nettuno. At any moment one or a dozen German planes might swoop out of the sun to lay a deadly trail of bombs and bullets ripping through buildings and bodies with sudden nerve-shattering sound.

The hidden horror of the beachhead was the constant presence of death. There were never very many casualties at any one time during the period of stalemate. But it was the constant waiting, the expectancy, that produced strain and tension. For every part of the beachhead was vulnerable to the reaper. There were no safe places. There was no refuge. And no one could forget this for long despite the grim jokes that tried to make light of the danger.

"Popcorn Pete," they called the German pilots who regu-larly dropped strings of antipersonnel bombs that crackled as they dispersed and fell to all corners of the beachhead. "Anzio Annie" or the "Anzio Express," they termed the 280-mm. railroad guns that emerged from a tunnel from time to time to throw shells that sounded like the roar of a train slamming down the tracks. They even had a name for the lone German reconnaissance plane that came over punctually every night—"Photo Joe."

To reduce the accuracy of German artillery and aircraft,

the Allies used smoke generators that created artificial fog. A whole series of smoke pots formed a semicircle paralleling the beachhead perimeter, others were placed on boats to screen the port. During the day the smoke generators produced a light haze, at night a dense low hanging cloud.

Though the liberal use of smoke made German artillery fire inaccurate and unobserved and forced German pilots to drop their bombs haphazardly, the protective smoke was disagreeable, terribly smelly and black and greasy, coating clothing, skin, and nostrils with a thin mask of carbonized oil that stifled breathing and made everybody feel dirty. The artificial fog and haze could not dissipate anxiety, for they could not obstruct the random shell, the lucky bomb. And finally, the screen of smoke that covered the face of the sun brought gloom to those who looked over their shoulders to see whether the next shell or bomb had their numbers on it.

To deal with emergencies brought on by air attack or long-range shellfire, the Anzio port commander had at his disposal special fire fighting personnel, rescue squads, a rescue launch, military police detachments, ambulances, litter parties, and a bomb disposal unit. He used them often.

That the Anzio port continued to operate at all was a testimonial to the quiet courage of those willing to work under these conditions. On March 29, when 7,828 tons of supplies were taken ashore, Anzio, in terms of unloading operations, was the fourth largest port in the world that day.

Still, the harassment of the shelling and bombardment provoked a nervousness beyond compare, particularly in the rear area where men were performing the usual noncombatant duties. Because soldiers broke down more frequently with what is called combat exhaustion, the medical authorities had to expand the capacity of those installations devoted to neuropsychiatric care.

What was it like back there in the rear areas? A partial report:

On February 8, German shells struck an ammunition dump, destroying 150 tons of ammunition.

On February 9, a German shell hit the 33rd Field Hospital, killing 2 nurses, wounding 3 officers and 3 enlisted men.

February 12, a bombing raid slightly damaged the 56th Evacuation Hospital and the 3rd Division Clearing Station, caused destruction in the 62nd Medical Battalion area and in an Ordnance installation—5 killed, 14 wounded.

February 13, shelling at midday along the waterfront interrupted unloading for half an hour—no casualties.

March 29, a shell hit a stack of C rations in a quartermaster dump.

March 30, ten and a half tons of ammunition destroyed by shells.

March 31, another ammunition dump struck—60 rounds lost.

April 1, three ammunition dumps hit by shells.

April 2, bombs destroyed 21,000 gallons of gasoline and a warehouse containing 30,000 pounds of flour.

April 3, heavy shelling of the port area damaged four cranes, destroyed 150,000 gallons of gasoline, 50 pounds of lubricants, and one ton of ammunition.

Between January 22 and March 12, antipersonnel bombs dropped from German planes killed 40 men and wounded 343. Two raids on March 17 killed 16 and wounded 100.

Early in April, German shells hit the Army post office, killing one clerk, injuring two others.

Even the medical installations, marked conspicuously by huge red crosses and usually respected by the combatants, were not immune in the congested beachhead.

February 9, the VI Corps Surgeon was killed.

February 13, two British Casualty Clearing Hospitals were bombed—3 killed, 4 injured, 5 ambulances destroyed.

March 22, about 40 rounds struck the hospital area—4 patients killed, 2 wounded.

March 29, bombs on the 56th and 93rd Evacuation Hospitals, 65 casualties.

April 5, two shells on the 56th Evacuation Hospital, 1 killed.

So it went. In four months the casualties among medical personnel alone totaled 92 killed (including 6 female nurses), 367 wounded, 79 missing and captured.

Everything in the beachhead had to go underground. Despite the high water table on the Anzio plain, great quantities of trenches, foxholes, dugouts, and pits protected men and matériel. Supply dumps were dispersed and frequently surrounded by earth bunkers. Bulldozers pushed tons of earth around neatly stacked piles of gasoline cans and ammunition. Engineers dug in all the hospitals, using dirt and sandbag revetments for all the tents, planking for shock wards and operating rooms. One division built two underground theaters, each capable of holding 200 men.

To keep the troops from going stale during the period of static warfare through most of March and all of April, a vigorous training program was necessary, as were rest and recreation. But there were no safe places on the beachhead for either. The units nevertheless did their best with training, and a large rest camp below Nettuno, also periodically under fire, provided facilities for swimming, movies, reading, and letter writing. Every four days a contingent of 750 men left by LST for a rest camp near Naples. Increased post exchange supplies, recreational equipment, better meals, and a steady flow of mail became extremely important for morale.

One of the most diverting occupations was listening to the radio. There were interesting programs on the Fifth Army Expeditionary Station. Even better was the entertainment offered by Axis Sally from Berlin—her throaty voice, her selections of the latest American popular tunes, and the crude, laughable propaganda she dispensed with the help of her partner George in vain attempts to promote despair and induce surrender.

What made life possible at Anzio in the midst of death was the logistical lifeline that pumped a steady stream of supplies to the beachhead. This operation, too, became an inalienable part of the accomplishment.

Despite hope for a relatively quick link-up between the Anzio force and the troops along the Cassino front, the planners had originally arranged a substantial supply effort in support of the landing. From ports in North Africa and from Naples, Liberty ships and LSTs and LCTs, some carrying pre-loaded trucks and DUKWs, brought the means of waging war and the necessities of life, plus some luxuries, for the men in the beachhead.

When the Germans contained the beachhead and made it an island or pocket of resistance, the Fifth Army logisticians devised a unique system of resupply. From January 28 on, weather permitting, a convoy of six LSTs departed from Naples every day on the 100-mile trip to Anzio. Each vessel carried 50 trucks, a total of 300 trucks per convoy. Each truck had been loaded to maximum capacity, then backed onto the ship for the voyage so it could be quickly driven off at the destination. The 1,500 tons of cargo carried in the trucks generally were 60 per cent ammunition, 20 per cent fuel, and 20 per cent rations. At Anzio, empty trucks had been assembled at the beaches ready to be driven aboard the empty LSTs for return to Naples.

Other vessels supplemented the daily LST shuttle. Each week fifteen LCTs made the round trip between Naples and Anzio. Every ten days four Liberty ships, usually loaded at North African ports, arrived at the beachhead, bringing not only supplies and individual troop replacements, but also special items such as wire, batteries, and the like.

At Anzio, LSTs and LCTs docked in the harbor, Liberty ships unloaded offshore, their cargoes brought into the harbor or over beaches by a fleet of twenty LCTs, almost 500 DUKWs, and a few LCIs. By February 1, the port was handling eight LSTs, eight LCTs, and fifteen LCIs simultaneously. A total of 201 LSTs and seven Liberty ships had been completely unloaded by that date. An example of the meaning of these figures is that by mid-February the Allies had almost 450 artillery pieces in the beachhead and all artillery weapons were firing an average of 20,000 total rounds per day.

The evacuation of casualties remained a problem until the coming of good weather. Since hospitals ships were unable to dock at the Anzio wharf, patients had to be ferried offshore by LCTs. Shallow-water beaches, gales, high seas, and enemy bombs and shells complicated the operation. Air evacuation was impossible because of the dust raised by the planes landing and taking off, which immediately brought artillery shells from the Germans.

Despite bad weather, poor unloading facilities, almost constant enemy air bombardment and artillery shelling, the Allies discharged more than 500,000 tons of supplies at Anzio during four months—a daily average of about 4,000 tons. There were no serious supply shortages. There was no impairment of tactical operations. There was no need for planners to worry about having to evacuate the beachhead.

Was it not, indeed, fortunate that General Lucas had looked after the logistical end of things so well?

THE BREAKOUT

9
DURING APRIL the Italian fronts were steeped in the ominous calm that precedes great battles. While the troops on both sides of the lines rested, trained, and regrouped, Kesselring and Alexander, each with twenty-two divisions in Italy, tried to divine what the other was likely to do.

Within essentially a defensive frame of reference, Kesselring was concerned about where he should place his mobile reserves, and to that end he tried to figure where the Allies would strike next. Which would be the diversion, and which the main effort? Would Alexander thrust across the Rapido or the Garigliano? Would he push out from the beachhead? Would he make amphibious landings at Gaeta, at the mouth of the Tiber, at Civitavecchia, at Leghorn? All were possible.

Like Kesselring, German commanders in all the other echelons ordered, demanded, pleaded with their troop units throughout the month for prisoners. "Just a couple, just one," so they might learn of Allied dispositions and intentions. Hitler attached great importance to the babbling of a Moroccan deserter. Much was made of a statement under narcosis of a wounded, captured British officer. German radio intercept teams studied Allied messages in great depth, trying to plumb information and fathom meaning as to where the Allies were likely to make their next move and how. All in vain.

While looking for some sign from the Allies, Kesselring improved his fortified lines of defense. In northern Italy about 50,000 Italian soldiers constructed a line anchored on the Apennines, while approximately 50,000 Italian civilians repaired railways and roads damaged by air bombardment. Between the Anzio beachhead and Rome, 10,000 Italians worked on the Caesar defenses, stringing an almost unbroken barbed wire barrier, in some places ninety feet deep, and digging gun pits and communication trenches across the southern slope of the Alban Hills. Kesselring thought he might be able to defend indefinitely at the Caesar position; Mackensen regarded it as strong enough for a temporary stand.

The extraordinary lull that hovered over the two separate fronts in Italy continued into the month of May. With no indications of an immediate resumption of offensive operations on the part of the Allies, Kesselring permitted some of his subordinates to go to Germany on leave. Vietinghoff, the Tenth Army commander, departed. So did the corps commander of the Cassino sector. Also off to Germany on convalescent leave went Westphal, who had not been feeling well.

Allied intelligence reports of what the Germans were likely to do in the near future remarked the enemy's defensive outlook:

The political and morale factors at home and among satellite nations, caused by a prolonged defense of Rome, and by successfully preventing the Allies from reaching and relieving the Anzio forces, are worth much to the Germans in view of continuing bad news elsewhere.

However great the propaganda value of sealing off the Allied landing and blocking our advance to Rome, large scale offensive action by the enemy in Southern Italy seems out of the question. At best the Germans can continue the stalemate. But new reliefs for this zone of operations are limited, the enemy's administrative problem will not diminish, and with commitments in other areas of Europe growing, Kesselring may yet not be able to avoid falling back and forming a single front.

The problem, then, was how to compel Kesselring to give up ground and abandon Rome. How best break the stalemate? Where should the Allies make their main effort when the time came to go over to the offense? Should they try to force a decision at the beachhead or at Cassino?

In facing these questions, the major Allied commanders in Italy, Alexander and Clark, came to different conclusions. Never completely together in their military thinking, they continued apart. Originally, Alexander had expected the Anzio force to be the compelling instrument in forcing the Germans to withdraw from Cassino, whereas Clark had seen the Anzio force as making an important assist to the decisive action at Cassino. Now, in the spring of 1944, they reversed their positions, Alexander coming to anticipate the important battle at Cassino, while Clark envisaged the significant action at Anzio. To these divergent ends, each commander applied his intelligence and energy.

As late as February 19, Clark had told General Wilson that as long as the Germans had six or seven divisions at the beachhead, it would be futile for the Allies to try to take the Alban Hills. Obviously the decisive move had to be made at Cassino. Yet ten days later, when Clark was relieved of responsibility for invading southern France, he was overjoyed, for, as he said, he had no time for anything except the battle of the beachhead. The focal point of decision, as far as he was concerned, had moved to Anzio.

During March and April, Clark built up the beachhead force. The 5th British Division went to Anzio to relieve the weary 56th, which returned to southern Italy. The 34th U. S. Division moved to Anzio and replaced the parachute regiment and parachute battalion. During March alone a total of 14,000 individual troop replacements arrived to fill the depleted ranks of the Anzio units. And finally, late in April, the remaining portion of the 1st Armored Division—Combat Command B, which had been waiting behind the Rapido for the chance to drive up the Liri valley—boarded LSTs and joined the troops in the beachhead. Truscott's VI Corps then had two British and four American divisions, a sizable striking force. Early in May Clark would give serious thought to sending another corps headquarters and two additional divisions to the beach-head, though he would finally send only one division, the 36th.

Alexander meanwhile was making important changes along the Cassino front. He recognized that nothing must go wrong at Anzio. For nothing, he said, could be worse for the OVER-LORD prospects than a catastrophe at the beachhead. But looking for the decisive move to be made at Cassino, he re-shuffled his forces there in wholesale fashion for a massive spring offensive.

Withdrawing the British X Corps from Clark's Fifth Army and leaving Clark with two corps, Alexander moved the Fifth Army to a zone only thirteen miles wide on the Italian west coast—the II U. S. Corps in the coastal area at the mouth of the Garigliano River with three divisions, the French Expeditionary Corps immediately inland with four divisions. Thinning out his Adriatic front, Alexander brought the British Eighth Army, now commanded by General Sir Oliver Leese, over to the Cassino area to take command of British, Canadian, Indian, Italian, New Zealand, and Polish troops—all concentrated for another crack at Cassino.

With both armies massed in a relatively narrow area entirely west of the Apennine Mountains in southern Italy, Alexander hoped to break through the Cassino defenses and into the Liri valley. The Eighth Army, facing the valley, which Alexander still considered the best route to Rome, was to make the main effort. The Fifth Army was to launch a subsidiary attack.

The first item on Alexander's agenda was a drive up the

Liri valley to make contact with Truscott's beachhead force. When juncture seemed imminent, Alexander would have Truscott strike out to the northeast through Cisterna to Valmontone to block Highway 6, the Tenth Army escape route. If Alexander could eliminate the Tenth Army by squeezing it between the VI Corps and the Eighth Army, he would find it easy enough to ride on to Rome.

In contrast with Alexander who was altogether optimistic about the prospects, Clark appeared quite depressed. He estimated it would be summer at least before the beachhead and Cassino forces could join hands and take Rome. And that, he believed, would be too late to contribute to the success of OVERLORD.

As part of the preparation for Alexander's spring offensive, Wilson launched a heavy air effort called Operation STRANGLE. To destroy the routes over which came German troops and supplies, Allied bombers attacked bridges, viaducts, and other communication bottlenecks for more than six weeks. About 50,000 sorties delivered 26,000 tons of bombs, making it unpleasant for the Germans to run the gantlet of air strikes south from Florence. A German captured later reported the main road below Florence "one tremendous military transport cemetery" with piles of wrecked vehicles lining both sides of the highway. By repeatedly bombing Italian truck factories at Milan and Turin, Allied pilots destroyed stocks of spare parts. As a result the overloaded Italian trucks used by the Germans, mostly Fiats, Spas, and Lancias, broke down frequently.

Yet the promises of the Allied airmen turned out to be no more than fond hopes. The mountainous terrain and bad weather were too much for the planes. The Germans were never critically short of rations or ammunition. Interruptions in the flow of supplies were only temporary. Like another Operation STRANGLE (how curious to repeat the code name) eight years later in Korea, Wilson's STRANGLE failed to choke the enemy's supply operations and cut the arteries nourishing the battlefield.

The shift of Alexander's troops from eastern to western Italy meanwhile was accomplished with considerably greater success. So skillfully, in fact, that the Germans remained unaware of the strength being massed against them, oblivious of the offensive intention.

While the Allied forces in Italy prepared for battle, Americans and British on the highest level of command continued to argue throughout March and April. Which was more important, invading southern France or pushing the Germans into northern Italy?

Prime Minister Churchill put the whole question into focus on April 13, as he wrote:

> We should above all defeat the German army south of Rome and join our own armies. Nothing should be grudged for this. We cannot tell how either the allied or enemy armies will emerge from the battle until it has been fought. It may be that the enemy will be thrown into disorder and that great opportunities of exploitation may be open. Or we may be checked and the enemy may continue to hold his positions south of Rome with his existing forces.

As a minimum endeavor, Churchill believed, the Allies had the duty of bringing relief to the beleaguered beachhead. Once this was accomplished, they could survey the situation again and decide what further tasks were most attractive.

The Americans agreed. Alexander's spring offensive in Italy would get first priority on the Mediterranean resources.

But the Americans did not accede to British requests for additional landing craft in the Mediterranean. The landing craft and ships that should have reverted long before to OVERLORD had, fortunately, not had the adverse effect on the cross-Channel preparations earlier envisioned. In this respect, the unopposed landing at Anzio had been a stroke of luck. The expected losses of boats and ships calculated by the planners had not occurred. But more important, somehow—exactly how was so complicated a process that it would never be fully understood except by a few logistical technicians—out of the global resources available to the Allies, the Combined Chiefs of Staff had found the necessary ships for the forthcoming invasion of northwest Europe. The long and unanticipated duration of the beachhead, the continued reliance of the Anzio force on water transport had not, in the final analysis, interfered with the cross-Channel arrangements. But beyond that the Americans would not go. They would make available no more vessels to the Mediterranean, especially since the invasion of southern France was in abeyance.

"History would never forgive [the Americans]," an enraged Brooke wrote in his diary, "for bargaining equipment against strategy and for trying to blackmail us into agreeing with them by holding the pistol of withdrawing craft at our heads."

Yet the issue as decided was favorable to the British point of view. All would be thrown into an offensive to be launched by Alexander at the Cassino line in May.

Alexander stated his intentions clearly. He was going "to destroy the right wing of the German Tenth Army; to drive what remains of it and the German Fourteenth Army north of Rome; and to pursue the enemy to the Rimini-Pisa line inflicting the maximum losses on him in the process." In the process, also, he intended to free Rome, which had become a symbol of success or failure to Germans and Allies alike.

Setting the attack for 11 P.M. on May 11, Alexander thus gave the troops two and a half hours after dark to move into their assault positions and an additional hour of darkness, before the moon rose, to launch their attack.

Alexander expected the Germans to fight stubbornly. But he was confident of the outcome of the struggle. He would drive the Germans back to the Rome area. He was sure that Kesselring would try to stabilize the front south of Rome on the Caesar line using all forces, including reserves. But he would overcome them there also.

Because he envisioned an important role for the VI Corps in unhinging the Caesar line, Alexander visited Anzio and conferred with Truscott six days before the scheduled date of the Cassino attack. He had already, late in April, instructed Clark not to use the two British divisions in the beachhead except in minor action because of the difficulty of securing individual troop replacements from a depleted England. The VI Corps offensive effort would thus be exclusively American.

On May 5 Alexander told Truscott to be ready to attack toward Valmontone, the only maneuver he thought would produce "worthwhile results." This course of action was consistent with Alexander's thinking from the very beginning of the Anzio operation, and it was in consonance with Churchill's concept. The Prime Minister was certain that the attack would produce "a decisive battle, fought to a finish, and having for its object the destruction and ruin of the armed force of the enemy south of Rome." Alexander would confirm "our object, namely, the destruction of the enemy south of Rome."

This thought followed the precepts of Clausewitz, who a century earlier had laid down the axiom that destroying the military forces of the enemy comprised the major task of warring elements. For Alexander and Churchill, an intermediate objective had to be attained before Rome. The prior need was to eliminate the German forces standing in the way.

But not for Clark. Rome remained his all-consuming interest.

Since Alexander had spelled out his views so specifically, there was really no room for decision at the army level. Yet Clark resolved to prevent the action of the VI Corps from being predetermined by a preconceived concept. He decided to use the corps himself in the most advantageous manner according to how he saw the situation developing.

Disturbed to learn that Alexander had bypassed his echelon of command and had gone directly to see Truscott, Clark made known his vexation. But he did not protest the substance of

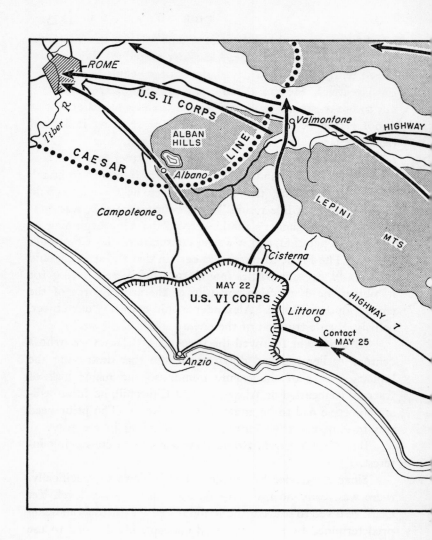

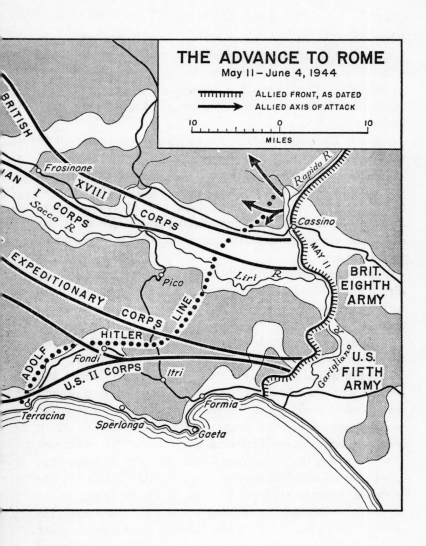

THE ADVANCE TO ROME
May 11 – June 4, 1944

ALLIED FRONT, AS DATED
ALLIED AXIS OF ATTACK

10   0   10
MILES

BRITISH

Frosinone

I CORPS

XVIII CORPS

Sacco R.

Rapido R.

Cassino

MAY 11

EXPEDITIONARY CORPS

Pico

LINE

Liri R.

BRIT. EIGHTH ARMY

HITLER

ADOLF

Fondi

U.S. II CORPS

Itri

Garigliano R.

U.S. FIFTH ARMY

Terracina

Sperlonga

Formia

Gaeta

Alexander's order. Suspicious that Alexander was trying to get the Eighth Army up the Liri valley and into Rome ahead of the Fifth, he told Alexander that he wished to keep Truscott flexible. What Clark wanted, it seemed, was to keep Truscott's mission indefinite and vague, like the original task he had given Lucas.

Clark doubted whether Truscott's limited forces could trap the Tenth Army, but he similarly questioned the advisability of turning the VI Corps toward Rome. He therefore deferred a decision. Despite Alexander's singleminded devotion to the Valmontone maneuver, which he had expounded at several conferences, Clark considered himself free to weigh alternative courses because Alexander had failed to issue a direct written order.

In the interest of flexibility, Clark suggested four different directions of attack to Truscott and told him to be ready on forty-eight hours' notice to take whichever became appropriate.

Truscott therefore drew four plans. CRAWDAD, a thrust northwestward along the coast, was discarded almost at once because it would contribute little to the spring offensive and because it would take the Allies over extremely broken ground that would benefit the defenders. GRASSHOPPER, a strike to the south to facilitate junction with the main Fifth Army forces coming up from Terracina, was disadvantageous because it would divert the corps from Rome and offer little opportunity to cut off withdrawing enemy troops. BUFFALO, a northeastward advance through Cisterna to Valmontone, would threaten the German Tenth Army withdrawal, but would produce a dangerous salient while leaving the Germans other escape routes beyond Valmontone. TURTLE, a northward move through Campoleone and Albano, would open Highway 7 into Rome, but would strike the strongest German positions along the Caesar line.

Of the four possibilities, two were practical. Despite Alexander's clear desire for Valmontone, Clark told Truscott to be ready to execute these two—a strike toward Valmontone to trap the Tenth Army or a drive north toward Albano to get to Rome.

Thus stood matters at 11 P.M., May 11, when more than 1,000 guns emplaced between Cassino and the sea roared out a furious cannonade to start Alexander's spring offensive in the south.

Polish troops assaulted Monte Cassino and fought bravely for more than twelve hours. But on the afternoon of May 12 they had to fall back, so battered that they would have to remain quiet for three days before they could endeavor again to take the abbey on the high ground.

At the Rapido, the front entrance into the Liri valley, British troops fought magnificently and crossed the river. But their bridgehead was so small that exploiting forces were unable to pass through for advance up the valley. Three more days of combat along the banks of the Rapido would be necessary before the British could expand their bridgehead and get into the valley proper.

Nor could the Americans of the II Corps, despite three days of bitter fighting, make progress in the coastal area at the mouth of the Garigliano.

It was the French who broke the Cassino line. Twenty-four hours of vicious attack by the French Expeditionary Corps, under General Alphonse Juin, smashed the German defenses in the mountains behind the Garigliano. Another day of slashing advance and French troops were standing on high ground overlooking the Liri valley from the south—several miles west of Cassino. One more day of pressure and the French had taken 1,000 prisoners and cut opposing German units to ribbons.

French success tugged along Americans and British. As the Germans in the coastal sector began to withdraw on May 14 to avoid being outflanked by the French, the Americans pushed forward, following the Germans closely. Fighting up Highway 7, the Americans would have no easy time, for German rearguards would be tough to overcome.

A day later, on May 15, the British were finally able to pass exploiting troops through an enlarged Rapido bridgehead and start up the Liri. By this time, on high ground overlooking the Liri from the south, six miles beyond the Rapido, French troops threatened the German withdrawal in the valley.

Bedeviled by these developments, Kesselring was helpless. His southern front was breaking, had indeed broken, but he dared not weaken his Anzio defenses because he expected the Allies at any moment to strike out of their perimeter. Nor could he draw additional forces from northern Italy because he expected Allied amphibious landings there. His headquarters had been attacked twice by Allied bombers on the morning of May 12 with damage to his communications. Allied planes had destroyed the Tenth Army headquarters. The world he had created was crumbling.

On May 16 Kesselring could no longer wait for events to right themselves. He could no longer hope for the Tenth Army alone to stem the Allied tide in southern Italy. He therefore moved one of his two best divisions, the 29th Panzer Grenadiers, from the Anzio area to reinforce the Tenth Army. He alerted Mackensen that additional units might have to be sent from the Fourteenth Army to the southern front.

Shifting the 29th Panzer Grenadiers came too late. Almost 10 miles beyond the Garigliano, French troops had already penetrated a second German defensive belt, sometimes called the Adolf Hitler line.

"The situation doesn't look any too good," the Tenth Army chief of staff, Colonel Fritz Wentzell, was telling Colonel Dietrich Beelitz of Kesselring's staff that day.

The remark was an understatement, as became quite clear when Wentzell proceeded to give a detailed account of Allied breakthroughs, Allied successes, Allied progress. Tanks were slashing through the mountains and destroying German positions and German troops.

Beelitz gave a low whistle. "Jesus Christ," he said. "I doubted that the enemy would be that strong."

"You don't know the French colonial troops," Wentzell said. "They are a bunch of roughnecks. Life means nothing to them."

The same might have been said about the Poles, for that night Polish troops again assaulted the high ground on which stood the ruined Abbey of Monte Cassino. The Germans fought fiercely. Though they would resist for two more days, the outcome of the battle was a foregone conclusion. The British were moving up the Liri valley and about to outflank Monte Cassino. That and the advance of the French, by then overlooking the Liri valley seven miles beyond Cassino, made the hilltop struggle for the abbey a rear-area engagement of little consequence.

In a vain attempt to stop the French, Kesselring brought down his other first-rate division, the 26th Panzer, from Anzio. Committing these troops also came too late. The 71st Division, bowled over by the French, had virtually disappeared. The 94th Division opposing the Americans was on the verge of disintegration as it fell back and relinquished the town of Formia, nine miles beyond the mouth of the Garigliano River. One regiment received orders to have the men scatter and make their way to the rear as best they could.

"I can tell you quite frankly," Kesselring expostulated to Wentzell that afternoon, "I can't call anything like that tactics."

But the pressure was too great. Seven to 10 miles behind the demolished Cassino defenses, the Adolf Hitler line, hastily renamed the Senger position after the corps commander directing the battle west of the Apennines, was about to fall.

To add to the trouble, Allied airplanes rained bombs on German logistical installations and troop areas.

Conversing on the telephone that day, Wentzell and Beelitz wondered what Alexander would do next. Would he invade northern Italy? Would he invade southern France? Northern Italy seemed the logical place for an Allied assault landing. "But if the enemy is planning anything up there," Wentzell mused, "I always ask myself, why are they trying so hard to destroy the harbors?"

Beelitz offered an explanation. "I think they are trying to interfere with our supplies."

On that day, May 17, Alexander and Clark were agreeing that progress on the southern front was creating conditions favorable for an attack from the beachhead soon. To Valmontone, of course, Alexander hardly needed to say.

Stressing the difficulties of driving to Valmontone, Clark suggested that the Valmontone maneuver might not be the decisive operation that Alexander expected. Should they defer selecting the axis of attack until the situation became even more clear?

Alexander thought not. He believed that the VI Corps could reach Valmontone and should do so. He also spelled out what he thought should be done beyond Valmontone—using light, mobile patrols, Truscott should try to cut other roads available to the Tenth Army for escape.

Clark was skeptical. Though the matter remained in abeyance for the moment, Alexander on May 18 informed Churchill that he would soon have the Americans at Anzio "punch out [to Valmontone] to get astride the enemy's communications to Rome."

On that day Vietinghoff, who had returned from a pleasant leave in Germany to take command of his Tenth Army in the midst of an inferno of Allied destruction, phoned Kesselring. If new units did not arrive quickly, he told Kesselring, he would soon have nothing left with which to oppose the Allies. One hundred infantrymen remained of the 71st Division. Supplies were disappearing. For example, one battalion commander who was wounded had fought until he and his men were out of ammunition; they then threw rocks until they were taken prisoner. Please, more troops, more men, more weapons, more supplies, please, for the Tenth Army.

Kesselring was sympathetic but powerless. If he took more resources from the Fourteenth Army at Anzio, he explained, he would "have to listen to Mackensen's reproaches."

By this time, as Wentzell explained to Beelitz, "Everything appears to be too late." It made no difference whether they called Allied progress a penetration or a breakthrough—"we are no longer able to contain the enemy."

The Abbey of Monte Cassino, long a symbol of German success and Allied failure, fell to Polish troops that day, and British soldiers entered the desolate pile of rubble that the town of Cassino had become. The Allied pressure that Kesselring had held back for five long months could no longer be denied. Allied forces swirled over the rock of the defensive position that had been the scene of some of the bloodiest fighting of World War II.

Twenty miles beyond the Garigliano, French units before noon of May 19 were across the Itri–Pico road, the main lateral highway connecting Highways 6 and 7 below Rome. The ancient fortress town of Gaeta fell to the Americans that day, as did the village of Itri, five miles beyond Formia.

With Allied troops 40 miles from the Anzio perimeter, it was time, Alexander told Clark, to think of breaking out of the beachhead. Not only had the Allies smashed the Cassino line, they had broken the Hitler line in the mountainous coastal area south of the Liri valley. But more important, Kesselring had weakened his beachhead defenses by committing reserves to stem the Allies in the south.

Clark procrastinated. An attack out of the beachhead was premature, he felt, until the British Eighth Army, lagging far behind the French, had at least moved up the Liri valley to the Hitler line. The British, in Clark's opinion, were making no real effort to drive hard, but were letting the French clear the way. Unless the British Eighth Army tied down the Tenth Army in the Liri, a VI Corps attack against the Fourteenth Army would have rough going.

But which way should Truscott go? Reluctantly, Clark decided he could not avoid conforming to Alexander's wish, at least initially. Yet if the situation developed favorably for an attack directly toward Rome, he would make that decision regardless of Alexander's conviction. He therefore instructed Truscott to be ready to attack through Cisterna toward Valmontone. But without notifying Alexander, Clark also told Truscott to be prepared to shift his main forces northward to Rome after taking Cisterna.

The town of Fondi, 8 miles beyond Itri, fell to the Americans on May 20 while the French drove toward Pico, threatening, if they took Pico, to trap the Tenth Army in the Liri valley. The Eighth Army, barely beyond Cassino, more than 10 miles in the rear, was regrouping to attack the Hitler line, still intact across the Liri.

The tempo of the Allied advance quickened on May 21 as a battalion of American infantrymen embarked at Gaeta in DUKWs in the morning and sailed more than 11 miles up the coast to Sperlonga, where they landed unopposed. Ten miles up the coast from Sperlonga was Terracina, the last stronghold where the Germans could possibly defend before the Pontine Marshes. Terracina had come into reach. So had junction with the beachhead.

On that day Clark told Truscott to start his attack toward Valmontone at six-thirty on the morning of May 23. Confident of the military outcome of the attack, Clark was concerned about the larger problems. He wanted to secure Rome before Eisenhower's D Day landing on the Normandy beaches crowded the Italian campaign off the front pages of the world's newspapers and out of the public eye. He did not think

Truscott could trap the Tenth Army at Valmontone. And he wanted to shift the VI Corps main effort northward into the Alban Hills and toward Rome rather than toward the head of the Liri valley. For he was determined that his Fifth Army and no one else was going to have the glory of capturing Rome. Too many American lives had been expended in Italy for anyone else to have the honor of taking the Eternal City. First he would have to obey Alexander. But he told Truscott to be ready for any eventuality, for any change in the direction of his attack.

At the beachhead the Allied troops holding the perimeter were, from left to right, the British 5th and 1st Divisions, the 45th and 34th U. S. Divisions, and the Canadian–American First Special Service Force. In corps reserve were the 3rd Infantry and 1st Armored Divisions, plus the 36th Infantry Division, which had just arrived.

On the other side of the front, the Germans had five divisions in the line—the 4th Parachute behind the Moletta River, the 65th astride the Albano road, the 3rd Panzer Grenadiers in the center, the 362nd at Cisterna, and the 715th along the Mussolini Canal. Behind them Mackensen had no reserves. The 26th Panzer Division had moved south and was opposing the French, and the 29th Panzer Grenadier Division, after moving south, had slipped over to oppose the Americans at Terracina. A gap opening between these two divisions had to be filled by part of the 3rd Panzer Grenadiers, pulled out of the Anzio front. Mackensen's nearest reserves were the newly activated 92nd Division, forming at Civitavecchia, and the Hermann Goering Division resting near Leghorn. Before he could use these forces, he would have to have Kesselring's permission.

The Germans had had ample time to construct field fortifications around the beachhead, and they had done a good job. Near Cisterna the forward line consisted of a series of platoon positions about 300 yards apart, each containing four to eight machine guns sited to fire a few inches above the ground. Wire had been laid, avenues of approach had been mined. Several hundred yards behind the forward line were reserve companies protected by dugouts along the ditches. Behind them were weapons pits and gun emplacements.

To break out of the beachhead, the Americans would have to attack uphill across the network of ditches and canals that wrinkled the face of the Anzio plain. At Cisterna the ground was fairly open and level, suitable for tanks. But beyond, in a 3-mile corridor leading to the upper end of the Liri valley at Valmontone, scattered patches of trees, vineyards, and wide, steep ravines cut by streams would slow an advance.

While the Allied forces in the beachhead prepared on May 22 for their attack, while American troops fought for Terracina and the French captured Pico, Kesselring made his strategic decision. Unable to put off the distasteful task any longer, he began a systematic withdrawal of the Tenth Army out of the Liri valley. German service units began to stream up Highway 6 and out of the valley through Valmontone.

At the beachhead at eight-thirty that evening, the British 1st Division launched a feint attack on the west side of the Albano road. At two-fifteen on the morning of May 23, the 5th British Division made an artillery demonstration along the lower Moletta River.

Daybreak came shortly after five-thirty on the morning of May 23, and with it came a light drizzle. In the Liri valley the British Eighth Army launched a three-corps assault against the Hitler line, already outflanked in the Fifth Army zone and lightly held by rearguards protecting the Tenth Army withdrawal. Around the beachhead perimeter more than 500 guns opened fire while sixty light bombers struck Cisterna to start Truscott's VI Corps attack.

The Eighth Army made little progress in the Liri. The beachhead attack achieved only slightly better results.

Truscott's assault gained surprise and should have ripped through the German defenses. For some half-awake and partially clothed German troops still in their dugouts were captured. German counterbattery fire was slow in starting. And German observers found the haze that lasted through the day frustrating. Though the Germans recovered quickly, they could never quite overcome their initial disorganization. Counterattacks launched during the day were nothing more than local in character.

Yet the VI Corps failed to make a striking advance. On the left of the main effort the 45th Division took limited objectives designed to hold the shoulder of the major penetration. In the principal attack toward Cisterna, barely 2 miles ahead, the 1st Armored Division on the north, the 3rd Division in the middle, and the First Special Service Force on the south passed through the 34th Division and had a difficult time fighting against the most tenacious resistance.

By the end of the day the Americans had reached the line of the Cisterna–Rome railroad, they had captured almost 1,500 prisoners. But they had lost about a hundred tanks and tank destroyers. The 3rd Division alone had sustained the staggering total of 950 casualties. And the troops were denied Cisterna.

Despite German success in holding both in the Liri valley and at the beachhead, events elsewhere foreshadowed an adjustment of Kesselring's defenses. Battling for Terracina against the II Corps, the units on the left flank of the Fourteenth Army had to fall back onto the flank of the Tenth Army. With both armies holding poor defensive positions in unsuitable terrain, Kesselring had no alternative but to move into the Caesar line. Before he could do so, he needed Hitler's O.K.

On May 24, as the II Corps took Terracina, a scant 30 miles from Cisterna across the indefensible Pontine Marshes, as the British continued their pressure against the Hitler line, as the French added their weight in the Lepini Mountains just below the Alban Hills, and as the VI Corps resumed its offensive toward Cisterna, Kesselring received permission from Hitler to pull his forces into the Caesar line.

On that day, though Cisterna still remained just out of

reach of the 3rd Division, tanks of the 1st Armored Division crossed Highway 7 north of Cisterna, and the First Special Service Force, bolstered by a regiment of the 34th Division, pushed beyond the railroad to Highway 7 south of Cisterna. Not only did these gains block the highway, but they opened a wedge between the Tenth and Fourteenth Armies. While Truscott was telling Harmon to go for Valmontone, Kesselring was bringing down the Hermann Goering Division and part of the 92nd Division to fight for Valmontone and Highway 6. The opposition in the valley leading from Cisterna to Valmontone began to increase, while inside Cisterna remnants of the 362nd held tenaciously to the rubble that remained of the town. "More opposition there than we thought," O'Daniel reported.

Events reached a climax on May 25. Shortly after daylight, American troops racing across the flat marshland from Terracina met an engineer patrol coming down Highway 7 from the north. The meeting achieved the primary objective of Alexander's spring offensive. Anzio was no longer a beachhead. Two weeks after the attack on the Cassino line, 125 days after the initial landing at Anzio, the two separate Allied fronts in southern Italy became one. The battle of Anzio, in effect, was over. But Anzio had never been more than an adjunct to the battle for Rome. And in that larger struggle, a final act remained to be played.

With Kesselring withdrawing the Tenth Army into the Caesar positions, the Eighth Army finally broke through the Hitler line at three different places on May 25. As the Germans marched northwest along Highway 6 toward Rome, the British followed and advanced toward Valmontone.

On that day also, the German resistance in Cisterna at last toppled, and the town passed into American hands. To gain Cisterna, the American units of the VI Corps had in three days lost 476 men killed, 2,321 wounded, and 75 missing, a total of 2,872 casualties. The British troops of the VI Corps, assisting by holding the I Parachute Corps in place, had lost 469 men. Against these losses, the VI Corps had taken 2,640 prisoners.

Though the VI Corps was now within striking distance of Valmontone, Clark remained interested in the shortest road to Rome across the western side of the Alban Hills. On the previous day he had asked Truscott whether the direction of his attack could be changed from the northeast to the north. Yes, of course, Truscott had said, but he thought that changing direction would be practical only if Kesselring reinforced Valmontone to such an extent that Truscott judged it impossible to take.

Clark was not at all sure of the soundness of this point of view. Alexander's long-standing idea of thrusting to Valmontone, Clark thought, was based on a false premise. Why would blocking Highway 6 annihilate the Tenth Army when so many other roads were available for the army's escape? Sending Truscott to Valmontone would impose a difficult maneuver on him—for to get to Rome from Valmontone, he would have to execute a complicated swing to the left in order to get astride Highway 6. Would it not be far better to strike at once up Highway 7 and directly into the Italian capital?

During the early afternoon of May 25 Clark could no longer delay his decision. Should he throw the entire weight of the VI Corps—five American divisions—toward Valmontone, should he turn the corps northward toward Rome, or should he strike simultaneously in both directions?

Despite the losses sustained in nearly three days of intensive action, Clark felt that the VI Corps was in good fighting shape. Overlooking the strength of the Caesar position at the base of the Alban Hills and the defensive capabilities of the three good divisions under the I Parachute Corps, Clark believed that the Germans were rapidly deteriorating. To him they appeared incapable of stopping the VI Corps no matter where Truscott struck.

Doubting that a drive to Valmontone would trap large enemy forces coming up from the south, Clark also concluded that a thrust to Valmontone was unnecessary to facilitate the Eighth Army advance. The Eighth Army had driven through the last German prepared positions on the southern front, and few enemy forces remained to impede the British. Why then encourage British competition for the capture of Rome? And why lead the VI Corps away from Rome rather than toward it?

Clark saw Rome as belonging rightly to his own Fifth Army. His army had taken the brunt of the campaigning in Italy. His army—the French were under his command—had made the decisive breakout on the southern front. In contrast, the British Eighth Army, despite Fifth Army assistance, had failed, in Clark's opinion, to capitalize on the German defeat. Though possessing the route that Alexander considered to be "the only way to Rome," the Eighth Army, Clark was certain, would not provide the strong frontal effort needed to trap the Germans. Without this, there was no justification for throwing the main strength of the VI Corps toward Valmontone.

If, as Clark believed, the bulk of the Tenth Army had withdrawn from the Liri valley; if, as he thought, the German forces before Rome were falling apart—the Germans could not hold back the VI Corps even though Truscott launched a direct thrust to Rome with less than maximum force.

Rome, of course, was the magnet. The capture of Rome would show the American people back home, as no amount of Tenth Army destruction would, tangible and dramatic evidence of American success in Italy after so much frustration. Suspecting that Alexander hoped to have the Eighth Army share in the triumph, Clark could not keep from taking the opportunity for a direct thrust that would make a sharing of the prize unnecessary. Besides, the cross-Channel invasion of France was imminent. Why delay in taking Rome? Why wait for the British? Why get involved in a battle to destroy an army?

Yet Clark could not entirely ignore Alexander's wishes. He had to continue toward Valmontone with some troops. For this reason, he split Truscott's forces. He ordered Truscott to drive on Valmontone with part of his units, while other units made the main thrust across the west side of the Alban Hills directly to Rome.

His decision made and passed on to General Brann, his Operations Officer, for transmittal to Truscott, Clark flew to his command post on the southern front to tell his chief of staff, Major General Alfred M. Gruenther. He wanted Gruenther to explain the operation to Alexander the next day, after the change in the attack had become irrevocable.

At about the same time, as Cisterna was passing into American possession and as the way to Valmontone seemed definitely open, Brann visited Truscott. "The Boss wants you to leave the 3rd Division and the Special Force to block Highway 6," Brann said, "and mount that assault you discussed with him to the north as soon as you can."

Surprised by the sudden change in plans, Truscott protested. He had no evidence, he said, that Kesselring had weakened his defenses in the Albano area. And this, he believed, was the only condition that would warrant shifting the direction of the main attack. Nor were there indications that Kesselring was concentrating forces in the Valmontone area in sufficient strength to block the VI Corps. It was no time, Truscott declared, to be displacing his strength to the north. The only logical thing for the corps to do, in Truscott's opinion, was to push on to Valmontone to insure the destruction of the Tenth Army. Could he talk to Clark before making changes in his attack?

Impossible. Clark was not at the beachhead. En route to the southern front, he could not, for the moment, be reached by telephone or by radio. He had instructed Truscott to attack to the north, Brann repeated, and there was no point in arguing. It was an order.

That settled it. Considering the congested area and the restricted roadnet available to the VI Corps, a more complicated plan was difficult for Truscott to imagine.

Having convinced Truscott of the necessity to change his attack, Brann radioed the Fifth Army headquarters. Truscott, he advised, was "entirely in accord."

Since there was no recourse but to act as ordered, Truscott telephoned somewhat later that afternoon to say that he thought "We should do it tomorrow."

Early that evening Clark returned to Anzio, where he conferred with Truscott and worked out the final details of the new attack plan. Clark then radioed to Gruenther:

I am launching this new attack with all speed possible in order to take advantage of the impetus of our advance and in order to overwhelm the enemy in what may be a demoralized condition at the present time. You can assure General Alexander this is an all-out attack. We are shooting the works.

Later that evening when Truscott called a meeting of his division commanders to announce the new plan, he presented the idea as his own. He appeared enthusiastic about its prospects, he showed confidence in its success. The 3rd Division, the First Special Service Force, and part of the 1st Armored Division were to continue northeastward to Valmontone while the 34th and 45th Divisions turned to the north toward Rome. The 36th Division in reserve between the diverging thrusts would free the bulk of the 1st Armored Division for the exploitation expected across the west side of the Alban Hills. "The Boche is badly disorganized, has a hodge-podge of units," Truscott told his division commanders, "and if we can drive as hard tomorrow as we have done the last three days, a great victory is in our grasp."

The division commanders were quizzical. They doubted

that the new thrust would break the German defenses at Albano. They felt that the shift was unjustified, particularly since Valmontone and Highway 6 had come within reach.

Facing the VI Corps in the east were the virtually destroyed 362nd Division and the severely mauled 715th, with contingents of the Hermann Goering and 92nd Divisions coming into the Valmontone corridor. Against the other part of the VI Corps in contrast were the 4th Parachute, 65th, and 3rd Panzer Grenadier Divisions—all veterans, all brought back to authorized strengths, and all still substantially intact.

But the decision had been made. Nothing remained except to carry out the order.

Although altering Alexander's scheme of maneuver, and diluting the strength of the force oriented on Valmontone, Clark gave no inkling of his intentions to his immediate superior. He had decided to act first and explain later.

Early on May 26 Clark confirmed his arrangements in writing:

The enemy forces opposing the beachhead in the Cisterna . . . area have been decisively defeated. The beachhead and main Fifth Army forces have joined. The overwhelming success of the current battle makes it possible to continue . . . [toward Valmontone] with powerful forces and to launch a new attack along the most direct route to Rome.

Yet the "powerful forces" thrusting to Valmontone had been robbed of their power and could not reach their objective against the increasing contingents of German forces blocking the way. As for the new attack in the Albano area that started at eleven o'clock on the morning of May 26, it was stopped cold.

Fifteen minutes later Alexander arrived at the Fifth Army command post and from Gruenther received the news of Clark's change of maneuver.

According to Gruenther's impression, Alexander appeared

"well pleased with the entire situation and was most complimentary in his reference to the Fifth Army" and to Clark. Far from objecting to the shift of the main attack, Alexander said, "I am for any line which the army commander believes will offer a chance to continue his present success." Yet he could not forgo asking Gruenther, "I am sure the army commander will continue to push toward Valmontone, won't he?"

"I assured him," Gruenther later reported to Clark, "that you had the situation thoroughly in mind and that he could depend on you to execute a vigorous plan with all the push in the world."

Alexander had accepted the explanation with his usual good grace. Gruenther was convinced that when Alexander departed he "left with no mental reservations as to the wisdom" of Clark's decision.

What else could he do? The new attack was an accomplished fact. And Alexander's acquiescence was strongly conditioned, if not determined, not only by Clark's success in the spring offensive, but by his previous relationship with the American army commander. He had no ground for questioning Clark's judgment on the best course of action in Clark's own zone of responsibility.

As events developed, Clark's decision neither unlocked the door to Rome nor cut the German withdrawal at Valmontone. At the Caesar line the Germans halted repeated, bloody, and fruitless efforts of the VI Corps to open Highway 7. Through Valmontone for more than a week the Tenth Army retired slowly, exposed and threatened but never trapped.

Ironically, had the VI Corps made its main effort toward Valmontone, Clark would have undoubtedly reached Rome more quickly by wheeling northwest there and swinging into Rome on Highway 6. He would certainly have put far greater pressure on the Tenth Army.

When Truscott finally broke through Kesselring's last defenses south of Rome, he did so by a surprise night infiltration along the eastern side of the Alban Hills between the two prongs of the attack. When this breach was widened, Clark turned his forces toward Rome and away from the withdrawing Tenth Army. With the British Eighth Army failing to keep heavy pressure against the Tenth Army, the Germans escaped.

On June 2 the Germans began to withdraw through Rome, leaving rearguards to impede the Americans. With the II Corps by then on Highway 6 at Valmontone and the VI Corps on Highway 7 at Albano, the divisions formed flying columns of tanks, tank destroyers, engineers, and infantry— usually a battalion or less of infantry and a company of tanks —to move into the city to secure the bridges. Behind them columns of infantry advanced on foot and by motor into the suburbs.

On June 4, while the Germans departed from Rome on the north and west along deserted streets, Americans entered Rome on roads from the south and east that were lined by cheering Italians. By midnight the Fifth Army stood at the Tiber. Every bridge was under guard. North and south of Rome, the Germans had destroyed the bridges, but in Rome itself all the crossings were intact.

The Allies had gained Rome, but they had not destroyed Kesselring's forces. Nor could they prevent Kesselring from making a masterful withdrawal 150 miles up the Italian boot. The Allies would follow in close pursuit for almost two months. Then, at the end of July, with Kesselring's forces behind the Arno River in northern Italy, the Allies would have to pause in order to consolidate their forces and make preparations for another battle.

But the future was not uppermost in Clark's mind on June 4, when the unsmiling but jubilant Fifth Army commander entered Rome. After all the frustration and pain during the nine months between Salerno and Rome, the great prize of the Italian campaign was finally his. It belonged to him and his Fifth Army.

The final act of the battle for Rome had taken its toll. Between April 1 and June 4, the Fifth Army had lost 35,000 men—21,000 Americans, 3,500 British, and 10,500 French, with most casualties having occurred after May 11. The Germans had suffered equally, prisoners alone amounting to more than 15,000, the Americans having captured 10,000, the British 100, and the French 5,000. The British Eighth Army lost about 6,000 men, took about 3,000 prisoners.

Two days after the liberation of Rome, when Allied forces under General Eisenhower assaulted the Normandy beaches to begin the liberation of northwest Europe, the campaign in Italy fell to less than secondary importance.

THE CONCLUSIONS

10

ROME IS about an hour's drive from Anzio, but in 1944 it took the Allies four months to get there. Across that landscape torn by shell and bomb, both armies left a trail of blood and agony.

For the Allies, Anzio had become an epic stand on a lonely beachhead. But this description could not obscure the heartache. The outcome of the landing was one of the great disappointments of the war. The amphibious assault did not produce the result expected, the quick capture of Rome. By the merciless logic of war, the operation was a failure.

What transformed imminent disaster into an achievement was the grim determination to hang on. What made it possible for the troops at Anzio to endure a situation frought with defeat was the logistical support they received. Without command of the sea the very concept of Anzio would have been out of the question. And in the end it was support across the sea, tied to courage on the battlefield, that turned implicit tragedy, despite the failure, into a victory of sorts.*

* "Naval gunfire, like air support," the eminent historian Samuel Eliot Morison has written, "was important . . . but not vital" in repelling the German counterattacks at Anzio. What stemmed the German offensives, he believed, was the "dogged valor of the American and British infantrymen and gunners. . . ."

Yet no one would deny the magnificent support, both material and

Boldly conceived, timidly executed—is this the right epitaph for Anzio? Was Lucas to blame for not taking advantage of the surprise he had gained? Or was he right to concentrate on his logistics?

Once Lucas decided it would be impossible for him to execute a swift *coup de grâce* against the Germans, his course of action was obviously correct. If he saw his force as too weak to make even a bluff, he had to resign himself to containment and confinement on a dangerous beachhead. He had to envisage a long defensive stand.

But it was precisely this prior decision that debilitated the vigor of the original idea. For the basic tenet of the Anzio ploy was a gamble. And in diluting the essential bluff Mark Clark must assume a major share of the blame.

Obsessed by dreams of glory—would he be the first to enter Rome from the south since Garibaldi? would he be the modern Belisarius?—he lacked the calculated madness required to stake his reputation on an operation that was too risky. He might gain Rome. But he might lose a corps. And in the final analysis, though he wished with all his heart that he might play the game, he judged the odds against him too great.

It was the British who wanted him to gamble. But he was the player who stood to lose. And it was, perhaps, the knowledge that it was their game that brought him increasing disenchantment with his allies who were at the same time his immediate superiors.

Sensitive to criticism, very sensitive of his prerogatives, Clark grumbled about British slowness, lack of flexibility, absence of aggressiveness. What he was grumbling about, par-

---

psychological, rendered the ground troops by the air and sea forces. Allied air losses are virtually impossible to assess, but the naval losses at Anzio were: for the British, 2 cruisers, 3 destroyers, 3 LSTs, 1 LCI, 1 hospital ship, 366 men killed and missing, 63 wounded; for the Americans, 1 minesweeper, 1 small minecraft, 1 LST, 2 LCIs, 3 LCTs, 2 Liberty ships, 160 men killed and missing, 166 wounded.

ticularly after Eisenhower's departure and the transfer of the executive direction of the theater from American to British control, was the framework of command that placed him under British supervision. It was galling that the British were calling the tune, and Clark was out of step. In this sense he was a much more tragic figure than Lucas.

Despite Clark's hard mask of imperviousness that concealed his sensibilities, he knew he was performing in a British show. But in the end he salvaged more than he might have anticipated. He gained Rome despite the scenario. He violated the rules, he changed the plot. He chose to gain an empty city rather than try to destroy an enemy army. Yet the violence and excitement of OVERLORD robbed him of the glory for more than a brief moment.

Alexander failed also. The Anzio concept was daring, but he was much too much the gentleman to make it work. A military commander in the tradition of Robert E. Lee, Alexander instructed his subordinates by suggestion rather than by direct order. He read the lines correctly, but he lacked the moral force to speak with conviction.

More than to any of these commanders, Anzio belongs to Winston Churchill. Somewhat like his ancestor, the Duke of Marlborough, who had won lasting fame at Blenheim, Churchill might have gained at Anzio comparable renown as a military strategist. But the men who carried out his bold gamble, for it was indeed *his* gamble, did not have the stuff to see it through. Churchill's Gallipoli of World War II, Anzio was not so catastrophic a failure, but was a blunder nonetheless.

Trying to put a good face on things, Churchill defended the maneuver that had gone astray. "Although the amphibious landing at Anzio and Nettuno did not immediately fructify as I had hoped when it was planned," he wrote Stalin on June 5, "it was a correct strategic move and brought its reward in the end." The battle, he explained, had drawn Germans into

Italy and had destroyed several of their divisions. This was enough, he maintained, to justify the anguish.

The trouble with Anzio was the extent of the gamble. Most military commanders are by nature careful, conservative, and conscientious. They deal in human lives and hard facts, and they are constantly oppressed by the necessity to make decisions that only God should make. From a sane military viewpoint, Anzio was impractical. Only an amateur would have pushed for its execution. And all the brilliance of the concept could not compensate for the deficiencies in the details.

The basic flaw in the maneuver, one that had disturbed all military professionals, was the distance between Cassino and Anzio. Anzio, as it turned out, but also as it was foreseen, had no tactical influence on Cassino. Neither front could support the other. By drawing upon the forces at the Cassino front, Anzio weakened the attack against the best defensive position in Italy.

The fundamental fault of the maneuver was the haste with which it was prepared and executed. The shadow of OVERLORD hung over Anzio. Because of OVERLORD's definite timetables, Anzio had to go before the cross-Channel attack or not at all. The landing craft available in the Mediterranean made it impossible to dispatch more forces to Anzio. But more ships alone would not have guaranteed more troops at Anzio, for additional troops could not be withdrawn from Cassino. Otherwise the main front would have been so weakened that the Germans might have successfully taken the offensive. Given the time span before OVERLORD, the leaders in the Mediterranean could not wait for either additional forces or more landing craft. The limited resources in Italy had to be carefully balanced, and OVERLORD precluded a change in the equilibrium.

Had there been no need for haste in launching Anzio, the Allies could have waited for the additional divisions from the

United States, North Africa, and the Middle East that turned the balance in May. More strength concentrated on the Cassino front might have prompted a breakthrough without a landing. Had Alexander reshuffled his forces in January or February as he did in April, he might have cracked the Cassino line. Had Clark reinforced the British penetration near the mouth of the Garigliano in mid-January, had he moved American troops into the British bridgehead before Kesselring's reserves arrived to seal off the breach, had he done this instead of trying to cross the Rapido directly into the Liri valley, the Fifth Army might have started to move. The army might have even got closer to the Frosinone area, perhaps to Frosinone itself, the place that planners had originally selected as the minimum distance from the Rome area acceptable for an amphibious landing.

Obviously, amphibious flanking movements were the best way to open up the situation in Italy, and everyone was aware of this. But the conditions were not ripe for a strategic envelopment of the scope that Anzio represented. Impatience on the part of a few frustrated commanders and the great persuasive power of a political leader overrode the technical objections of career soldiers who were uncomfortable with a gamble of such magnitude.

It was more than the disastrous rehearsal a few days before Anzio that prompted Truscott, then the 3rd Division commander, to protest the operation in a note to General Gruenther. "I believe that you know me well enough," Truscott wrote, "to know that I would not make such a point unless I actually felt *strongly* about it. If this is to be a 'forlorn hope' or a 'suicide sashay' then all I want to know is that fact —— If so, I'm positive that there is no outfit in the world that can do it better than me—even though I reserve the right (personally) to believe we might deserve a better fate."

For the Germans too, Anzio was a failure. The long

battle, the long stalemate meant failure for the Germans as for the Allies.

Hitler had assumed that the Allies would invade northwest Europe in a single main effort, and all signs pointed to a cross-Channel endeavor. Yet the large Allied forces in the Mediterranean led him to wonder whether other major thrusts, perhaps in Portugal or the Balkans, might precede or accompany the main blow. Believing it hardly likely that the Allies would push all the way up the Italian peninsula, he viewed the accumulated Allied power in the Mediterranean and the comparative stalemate in Italy as a strategic imbalance that the Allies might try to resolve by another sudden major assault.

Anzio seemed to confirm Hitler's theory. The Anzio beachhead appeared to have only remote tactical connection with the main front. Was it therefore an independent, self-sustaining operation, the first of a series of attacks on the continental periphery designed to disperse German reserves? The surprising fact that the Allies did not push inland from the Anzio beaches, but paused to consolidate their beachhead lent validity to Hitler's interpretation. For the purpose of the operation seemed not to be to gain tactical objectives but rather to attract German forces. Seeing the Allies executing what he took to be a peripheral strategy, Hitler began to expect attacks in Portugal, against the western and southern coasts of France, and in the Aegean before the main assault struck the beaches of northwest France.

Despite his estimate, Hitler reacted to Anzio in force and fury, not so much because he cared whether it might represent the first of a series of major amphibious assaults, but because he saw the possibility of obtaining political prestige by wiping out at least this beachhead. By authorizing reinforcements to move from southern France, Yugoslavia, and Germany, Hitler gambled. He lost, perhaps because his gamble was halfhearted. He could not afford to expose further the vulnerable areas where the Allies might strike next.

Had Hitler won at Anzio, he might have profoundly changed the course of the war. By driving the Allies into the sea, he would have gained at least a temporary respite from the Allied strategic stranglehold. He could have lightened his troop strength in Italy and bolstered his Atlantic Wall—to the point perhaps of stopping the Normandy invasion. He might even have gained enough time—though this rests on the outer edge of speculation—to conclude a negotiated peace.

Kesselring's tactical failure to eradicate the Anzio abscess —was he deprived of victory by Mackensen's caution?—made it easier for the Allies to succeed in Normandy. Rommel had always felt that it was impossible to dislodge invading troops once they had dug in on a beachhead—Sicily and Salerno were good indications—and Anzio confirmed his belief. Rommel would be opposing the Allies in Normandy, and when he would see the initial assault troops through his Atlantic Wall, he would despair of eventual German triumph.

Anzio taught the Allies two immediate lessons, both heeded in OVERLORD—more strength in the initial landing and an immediate drive to key points inland. The beachhead also demonstrated the importance of maintaining lifelines across the water. Together with experience in World War I, as well as a host of operations during World War II, Anzio reiterated—as Korea would further show—that relatively small and isolated forces can survive. As the shadow of atomic warfare hovers over the future and presages the wide dispersal of troops, task forces like the one at Anzio will no doubt depend for nourishment on the ability of ships or other forms of transport to carry to them the material substance of life along with the intangible elements of hope and faith.

What if Anzio had immediately succeeded in driving the Germans north of Rome? Would the shock to the Germans have facilitated the invasion of Normandy?—quickened the tempo of the war and brought its end more rapidly? Undoubtedly.

Would quick success at Anzio have pulled the Allies into the Balkans? Perhaps. But certainly not without violent prior strategic argument between the Allies. Despite talk in the Mediterranean theater and in London of operations into the Balkans, despite the existence in the official files of a few tentative studies of Balkan opportunities, prospects, and disadvantages, there is no evidence of a firm desire on Churchill's part (or of anyone else's) for a Balkan adventure. Perhaps the decisive reason for Churchill's reticence in 1943 and most of 1944 was his appreciation of the firm American opposition that a plan of this sort would encounter. But what seems more likely is that the benefits of entering the Balkans in order to checkmate the Russians became much clearer in retrospect after the war. In early 1944 the Allies were looking toward OVERLORD and western Europe.

And what of the Italian campaign itself? Was the expenditure of lives in the dreadful conditions of southern Italy justified? Should the Allies have concentrated elsewhere? From within the context of the strategic thinking of the time, it is difficult to see where else the Allies could practically and realistically have fought the Germans. Fight them, they had to, as Churchill made clear. Pin them down, they did. If the Allies can be criticized, it is that they tried to do too much in Italy with too little, and this they did because they had no other choice.

Given the virtual equality of losses suffered in Italy by both sides, the casualties incurred by the Germans were proportionately more severe. On that basis alone the campaign was warranted. But more, on that campaign was predicated the Italian surrender, a major Allied triumph. And perhaps worth considering is the stream of Allied observers, officers of high rank who came to Italy to learn how the war was being fought and who profited from the lessons, as the victories in France later demonstrated.

When the Allied forces in Italy moved north of Rome in

pursuit of the retreating Germans, one of the major conditions for an invasion of southern France was met. On August 15, three American divisions under Truscott's VI Corps, the First Special Service Force, British paratroopers, and French units, all under Lieutenant General Alexander M. Patch's Seventh U. S. Army, invaded the Mediterranean shore of France. The forces opened the ports of Marseilles and Toulon and drove up the Rhone valley to eventual juncture with Eisenhower's OVERLORD forces.

If Anzio had never taken place, if the front in Italy had remained south of Rome during the spring of 1944, the Allied leaders in the Mediterranean theater would probably have invaded southern France nevertheless. Had they made this decision, they would have made their landing to coincide with the cross-Channel attack. This would probably have deprived the Allies in Italy of the strength required to take Rome. But they could have continued to pin down the Germans in Italy. And more important, as Eisenhower and other American strategists later felt, a subsidiary invasion in the south of France would have facilitated OVERLORD and subsequent progress from the Normandy beaches. A double invasion of France might have prompted the Germans to loosen their hold on Normandy more quickly and with less pain. The battle of the hedgerows, the battles of Caen and Saint-Lô might never have occurred had Allied troops in southern France threatened the German rear from the first.

In southern France, after enough French troops had been brought from North Africa to form the First French Army under General de Lattre de Tassigny, General Devers, on September 15, took command of the Sixth Army Group with French and Seventh Armies under him. Had General Clark not elected to remain in Italy, a choice forced upon him by the existence of the Anzio beachhead, he would undoubtedly have been promoted to the Sixth Army Group command. He would thus, together with Bradley and Montgomery, have participated in the main Allied effort directed by Eisenhower against the heart of Germany. Instead, Clark stayed in Italy for the remainder of the war.

Clark was, nevertheless, to have his promotion to army group commander. Upon the death of Field Marshal Sir John Dill, the permanent representative in Washington of the British Chiefs of Staff, General Wilson was transferred to take his place in the late fall of 1944. Alexander in turn was elevated to the theater command, and Clark moved up to his position. Truscott then returned to Italy to assume command of the Fifth Army.

The campaign in Italy continued inexorably up the peninsula. During the last days of April, 1945, the resistance finally disintegrated. At the beginning of May, several days before the over-all German surrender, the Germans in Italy capitulated. Less than two months earlier, in March, in a futile attempt to avert defeat there, Hitler had transferred to the western front Kesselring, whose generalship in Italy had made him one of the great commanders of the war.

When American troops of the Fifth Army met soldiers of the Seventh Army coming from Austria in the Brenner Pass, one of the largest pincer movements in the history of warfare was complete. In this perspective, Anzio appears only as a small episode, though probably the most dramatic event, of the Italian campaign. Anzio had little effect on the outcome of the war. It gave the Allies no swift victory. Nor did it persuade the Germans of their eventual defeat.

For both adversaries, Anzio was no more than a gamble that failed.

AUTHOR'S NOTE

IN ADDITION to the official records of World War II to be found in the National Archives, the following works are the major sources for Anzio: (1) The Fifth Army *History*, written by members of the Fifth Army Historical Section immediately after the war and printed in Italy, is a straightforward narrative supplemented by valuable maps, charts, and statistics; volumes IV and V are pertinent. (2) A pamphlet prepared by the Army's Historical Division, published shortly after the war in the AMERICAN FORCES IN ACTION series, and entitled *Anzio* is excellent for its tactical detail. (3) Wynford Vaughan-Thomas's *Anzio* (New York: Holt, Rinehart, and Winston, 1961) is a superb presentation of the battle from a British point of view. (4) Three essays in *Command Decisions*, edited by Kent Roberts Greenfield (New York: Harcourt, Brace, 1959), are important—Ralph S. Mavrogordato's "Hitler's Decision on the Defense of Italy," Sidney T. Mathews' "General Clark's Decision to Drive on Rome," and my own "General Lucas at Anzio." (5) Memoirs include Winston S. Churchill's *Closing the Ring* (Boston: Houghton Mifflin, 1951), Mark W. Clark's *Calculated Risk* (New York: Harper, 1950), Lucian K. Truscott, Jr.'s *Command Missions* (New York: Dutton, 1954), Albert Kesselring's *A Soldier's Record* (New York: Morrow, 1954), and Siegfried Westphal's *The German Army in the West* (London: Cassell, 1951).

I wish to thank two former Chiefs of the Army's Office of Military History, Brigadier General James A. Norell and Brigadier General William H. Harris, for their interest in this project. I extend my thanks to Mr. Hanson W. Baldwin, the editor of the series, and to Mr. Stewart Richardson of Lippincott. And I acknowledge with gratitude the guidance and help of my friend, Mr. Charles B. MacDonald.

The opinions, conclusions, and interpretations expressed in this book are mine alone.

M. B.

INDEX